折り紙建築
ORIGAMIC ARCHITECTURE

Author

Masahiro CHATANI

1934	born in Hiroshima
1949～1952	Hibiya high school
1952～1956	Tokyo Institute of Technology
1956～1961	Design Dept. of Taisei Construction Co.
1961～1969	Building Research Institute, Ministry of Construction
1967	Doctor of Engineering
1969～1980	Associate Professor of Tokyo Institute of Technology
1977	Visiting Associate Professor of University of Washington, Seattle
1980～	Professor of Tokyo Institute of Technology
1981	Director of Japan Architects Association
1983	Director of Japanese Institute of Architecture, Chief editor

Exhibition of Origamic Architecture

1982	Design Gallery, Matsuya, Ginza, Tokyo
1983	Tokyo——Aoyama, Kichijoji, Waseda, Ikebukuro
	Shizuoka
	Nagoya
	Nagasaki

ORIGAMIC ARCHITECTURE OF MASAHIRO CHATANI

Published by SHOKOKUSHA Publishing Company Ltd.
25 Sakamachi, Shinjuku-ku, Tokyo, Japan
Printed in Japan
8th Printing 1984
ISBN4-395-27011-5 C3072

折り紙建築

オリガミック・アーキテクチャー

ORIGAMIC ARCHITECTURE OF MASAHIRO CHATANI

茶谷正洋

彰国社

An Invitation

Masahiro Chatani

Welcome to my mysterious world of Origamic creation! Look! Here are some white postcards. Try to open one. Magically, as the paper comes apart, it takes form. This is my world of architectural fantasy! Though inspired by traditional Origami, or folded paper, it is neither folded, nor cut paper but a 20th century version of the children's pop up book. It explores the mystery of transformation from the 2-dimensional plane to 3-dimensions taking into account the dimension of time. I call it **Origamic Architecture**.

Although of the computer age, Origamic experience is not of the computer but of human imagination.

In "Edo Period" Japan, the "Okoshi-e" or folding paper model was used to design tea houses. Origamic Architecture may be considered a development from the Okoshi-e, from Origami and from the joy of children playing with simple toys.

Origamic Architecture may also be considered as a bridge between the ancient and the modern times and between the cultures of East and West. The pieces range from explorations of 90°, 180° and 360° rotations. They also include the creation of the visual illusion of 3-dimensional form in 2-dimensions using the same vocabulary of folding and cutting cards.

These forms are created for enjoyment, exploration and participation. Touch them, move them, bring them alive, enjoy them, encounter them and understand them. They cannot be properly understood until you have made them part of your experience!

前口上

さあお立ち会い，ここに取りいだしましたるは，ただの二つ折り葉書大の白いケント紙。そろりと開いてみればあーら不思議，にゅうっと動いて飛び出す，折り紙とも切り紙ともつかぬ造形だ。建築メルヘンだ。紅毛碧眼向けに名づけたオリガミック・アーキテクチャー(折り紙建築)，これぞ二十一世紀を目指すポップ・アップ絵本ならぬ図本，ペッタンコの二次元平面から生まれる三次元立体の妙，開くにつれて時々刻々と形の変化する様はコンピューターにも描けない美しさ？

そのむかし，お茶室の起し絵があったっけ。

お持ち遊ぶの由来通り，これが本家のおもちゃというものだ。

世界中の建築が出てくるよ。古今東西森羅万象，創造物は何でも見立てて作れるんだ。まだある。カタカナ，ひらがな，漢字に英語，90°の角度に開くのから，180°，360°，いろいろそろって0°の型まで出来ちゃった。

さあさ寄ってらっしゃい，見てらっしゃい。お目にとまったのも何かの縁，本当は写真じゃわからねえ，作ってみなよ，みなの衆。滅法面白いんだぜ，折り紙付き！

頓首

目　次　Contents

協力	茶谷研究室	中谷　仁	**Associates**	Jin Nakatani
		中野晶子		Akiko Nakano
		ベンジャミン・ワーナー		Benjamin Warner
撮影	彰国社写真部	和木　通	**Photo**	Tohru Waki

I Opening 展(ひら)く

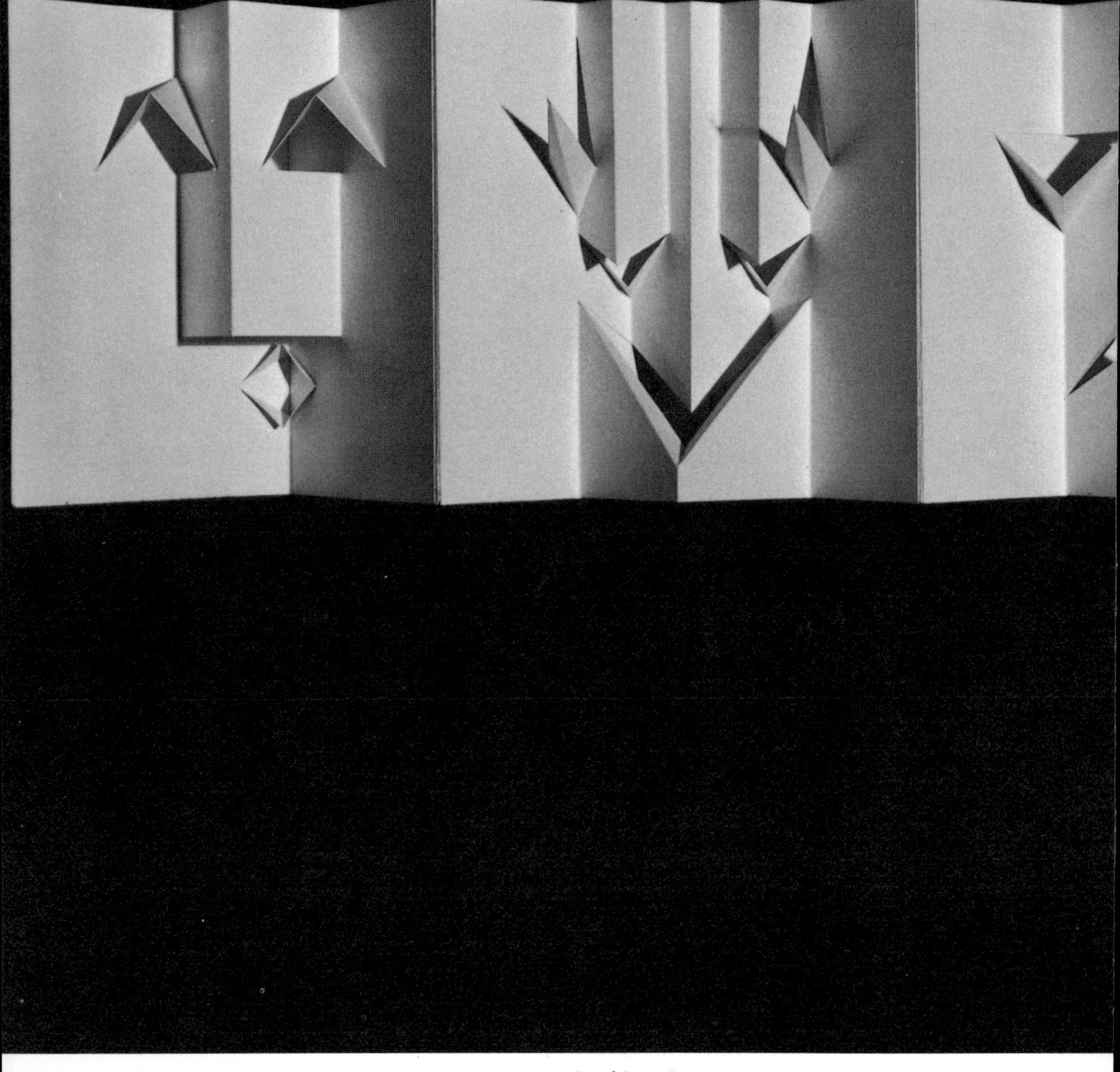

1 喜　Happiness

2 怒　Anger
3 哀　Grief

4 楽 Pleasure

5 へのへのもへじ Letraface

6　エッシャーの家 1　Escher House 1

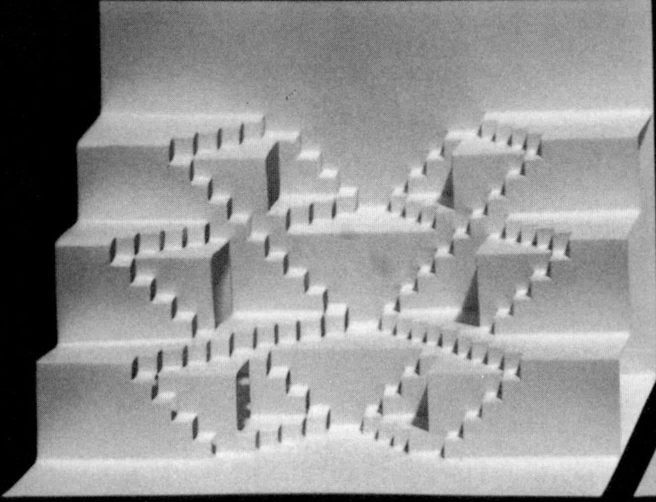

7　エッシャーの家2　Escher House 2

8　白い舞台　White stage

9　ブロック　Block

10　蜂の巣　Honeycomb

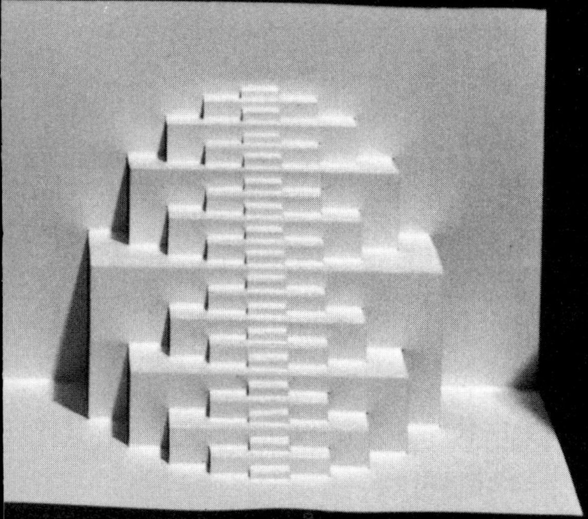

11　**マヤの階段**　Mayan pyramid
12　**貝の音階**　Shell music
13　**十三階段**　Stairway to hell

●パターン シリーズ　Pattern series

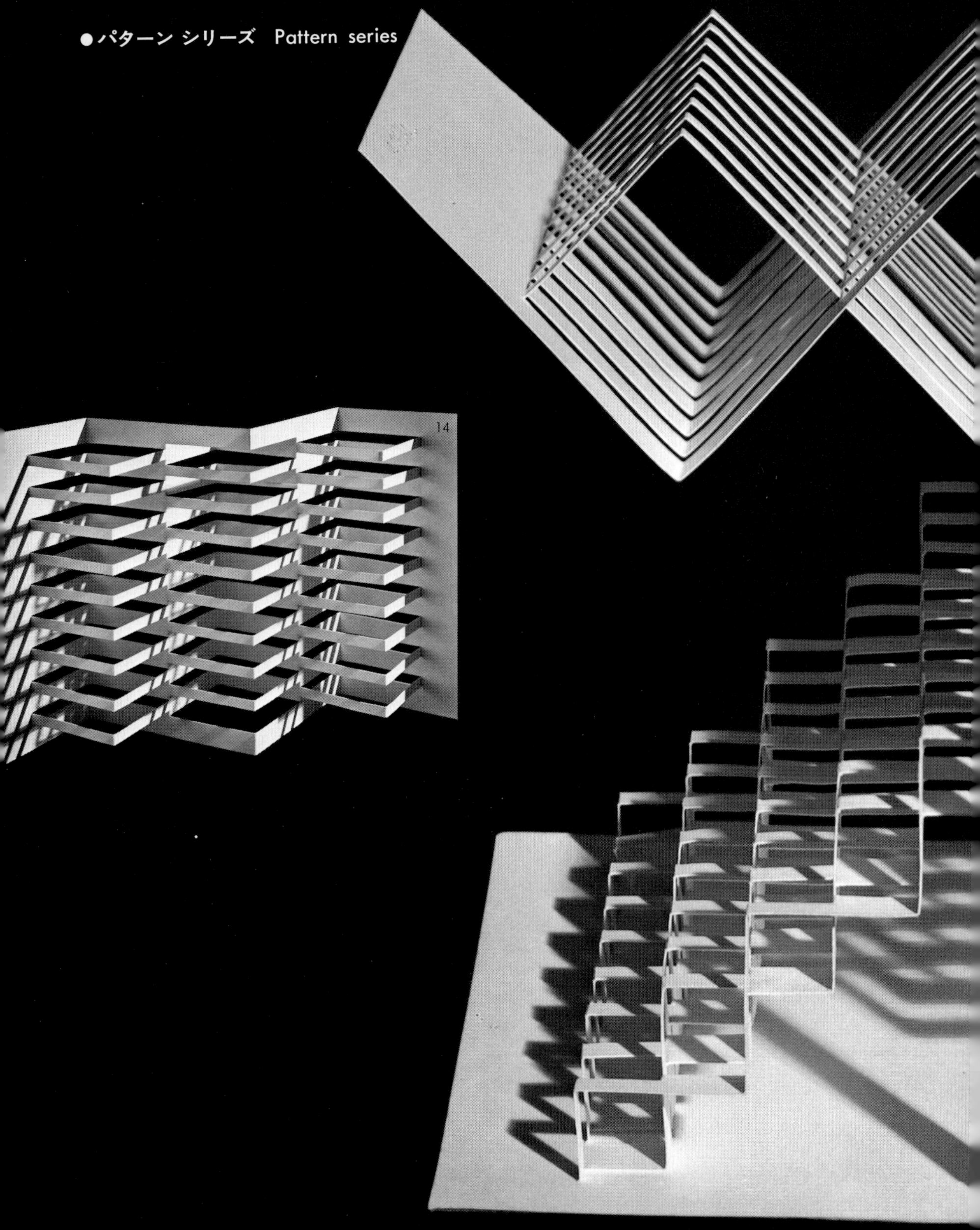

14　すだれ　Screen

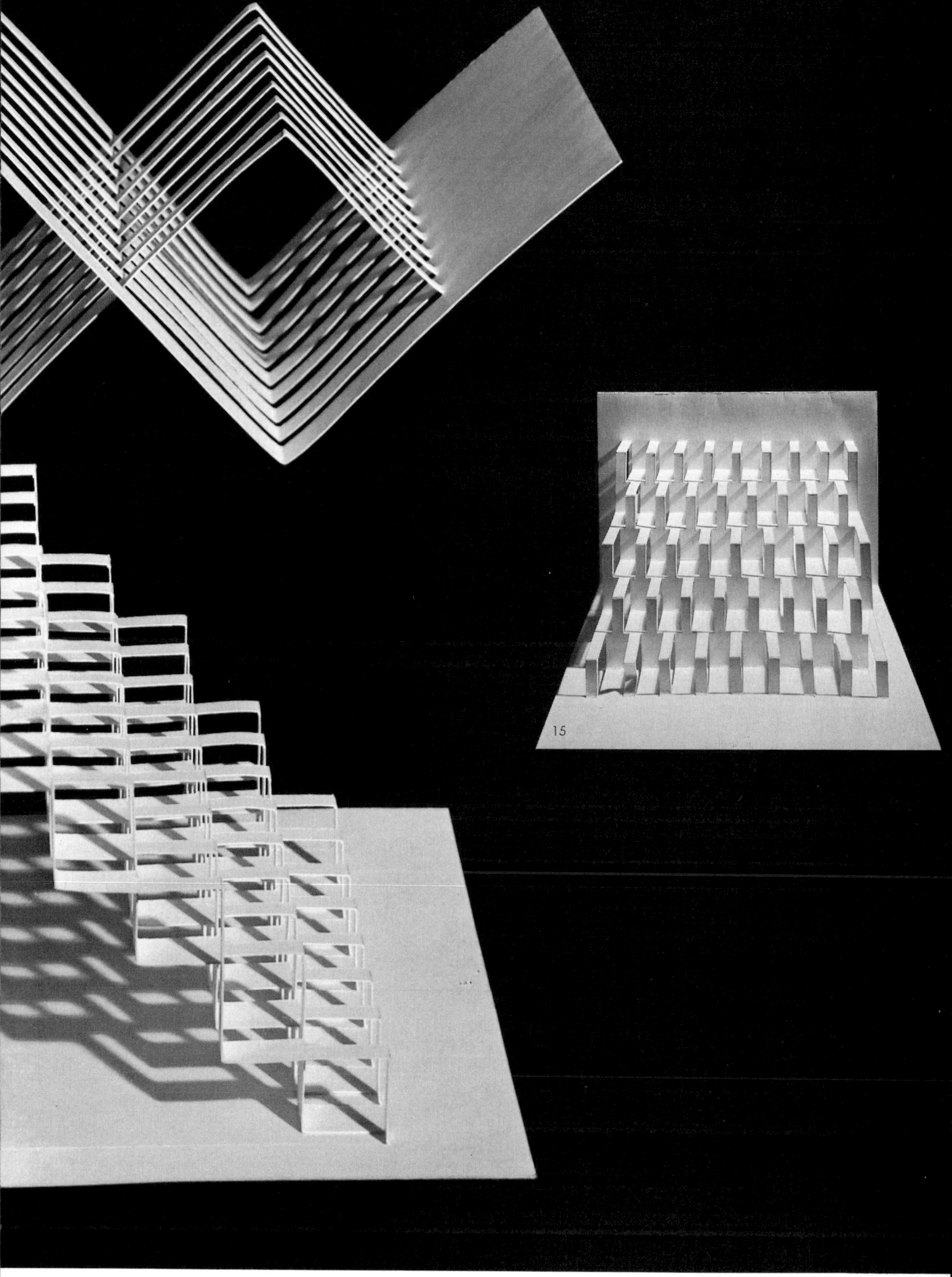

15　矢がすり　Slit and arrow

16 アフリカの家 African hut
17 タージマハール Taj Mahal
18 ロンドンの下町 London rowhouses
19 パルテノン Parthenon

20　十字ヶ丘の分譲地 Necropolis

21　ミコノス Mikonos

22　アムステルダム Amsterdam façade

23　オルガン教会 Organ church

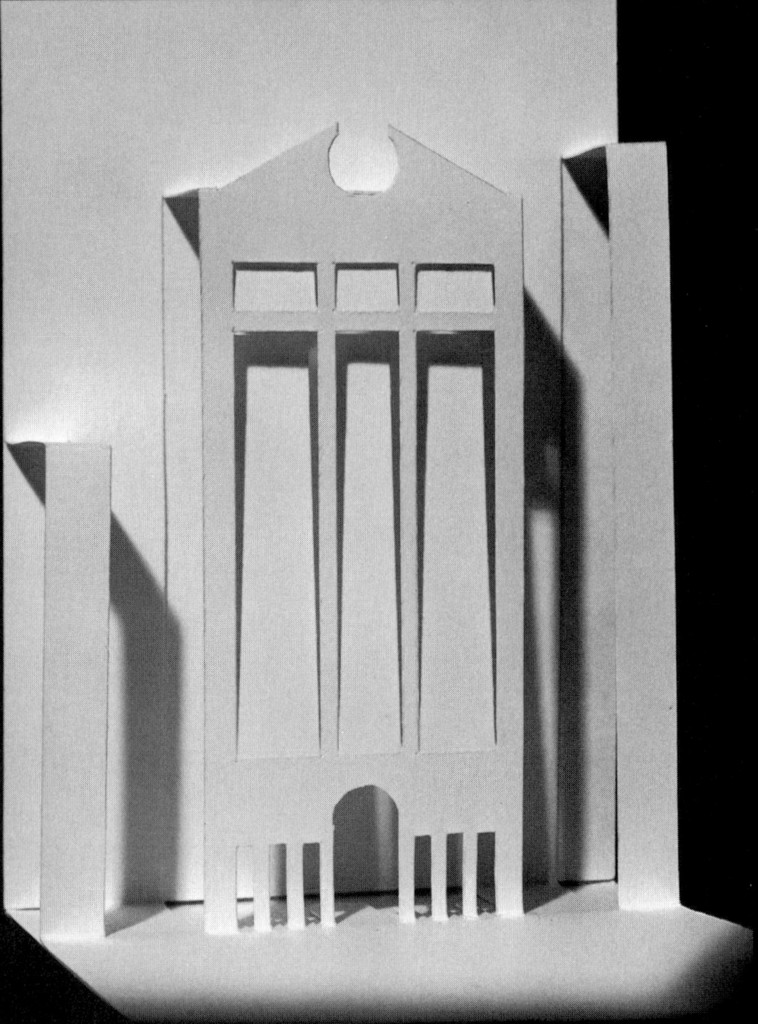

24 ポストモダン Post modern

25 ガラスのピラミッド Glass pyramid

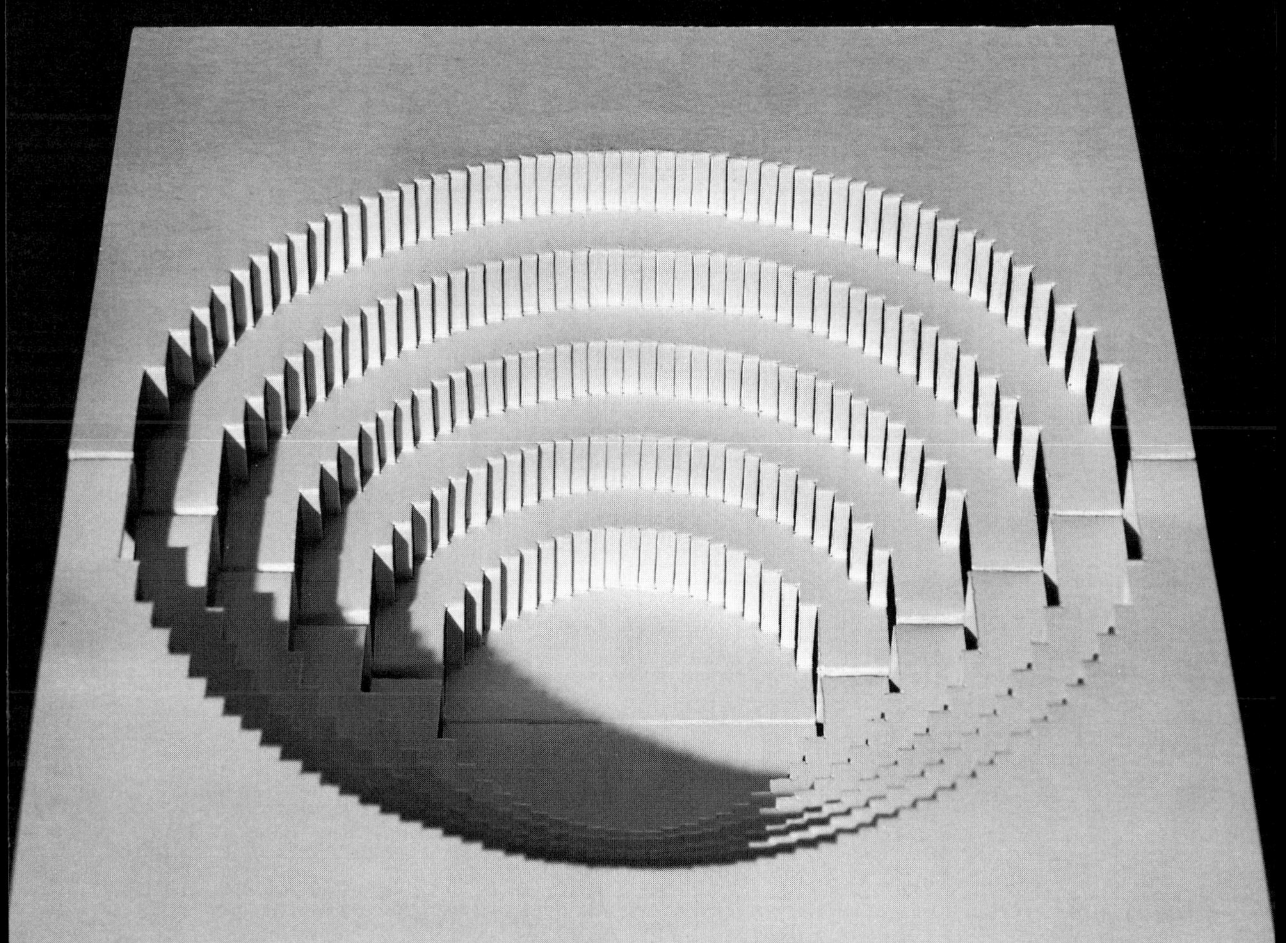

26　ウェディングパレス　Wedding palace　　27　円型劇場　Amphitheatre

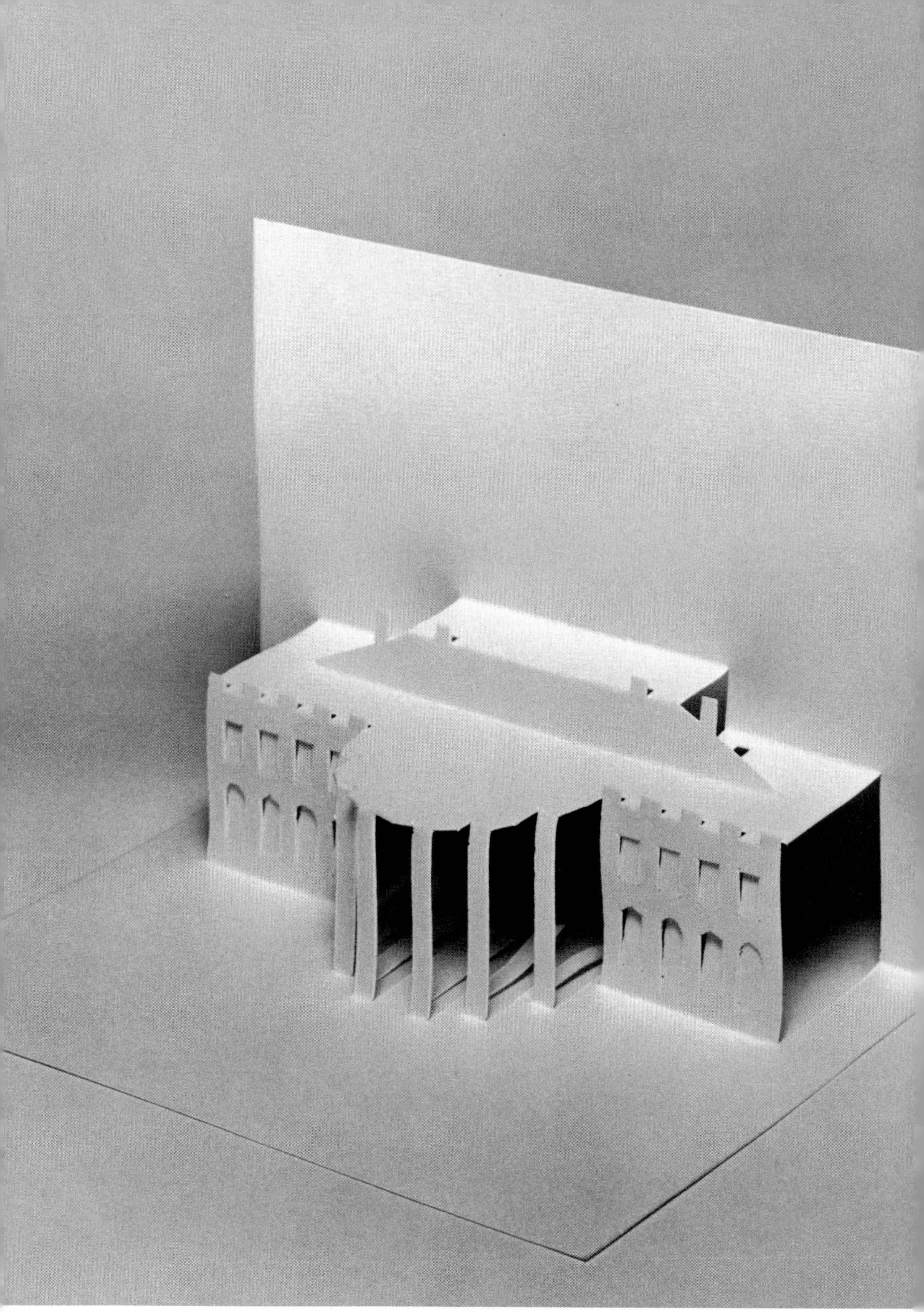

28　ホワイトハウス1　The White House 1

29　ホワイトハウス2　The White House 2

●穴の家シリーズ
Cave series

32

30　崖の家　Cliff house

32　地下の家１　Underground house 1

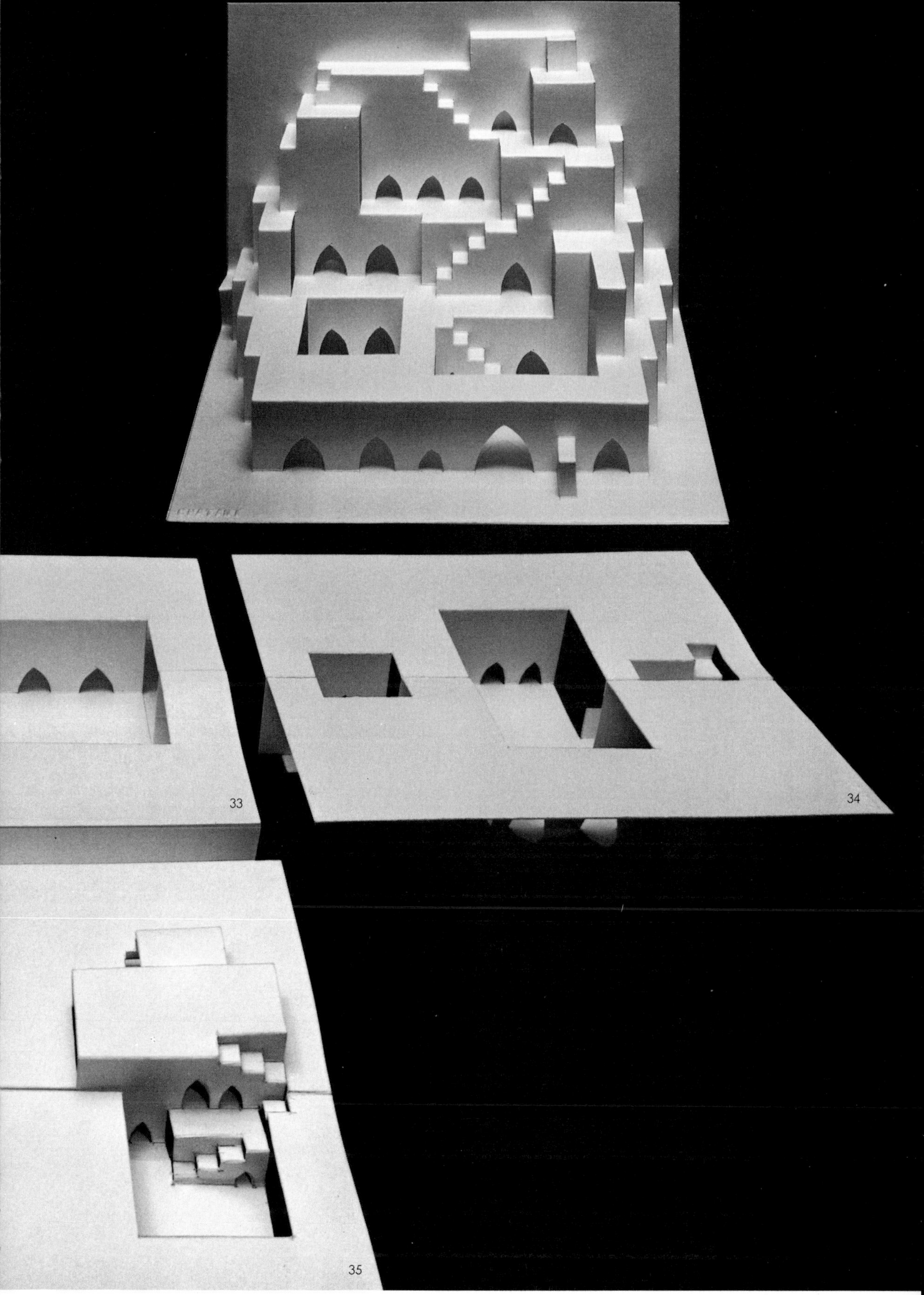

31 **龍宮城** Palace of the seagoddess
33 **地下の家2** Underground house 2
34 **地下の家3** Underground house 3
35 **地下の家4** Underground house 4

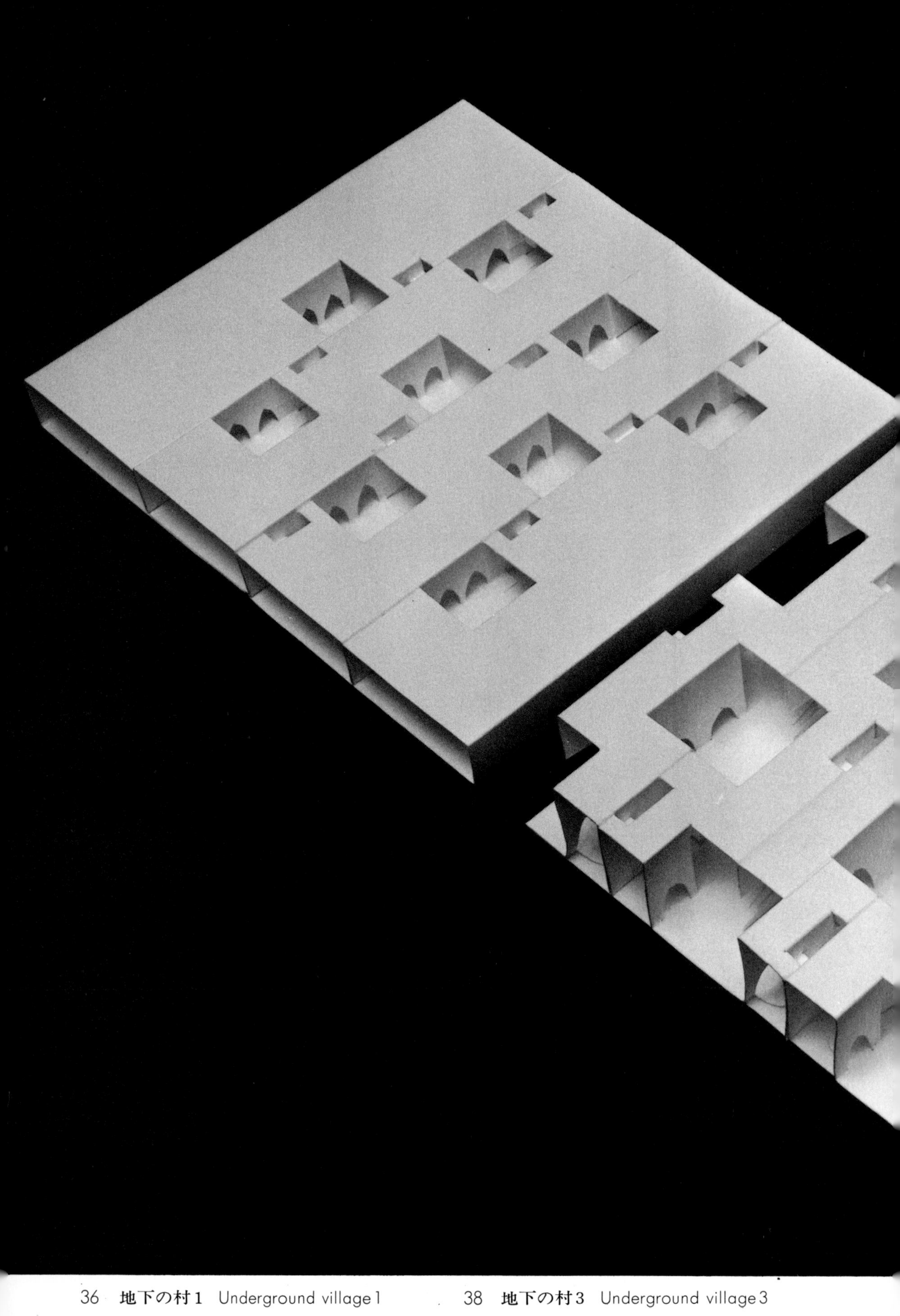

36　**地下の村 1**　Underground village 1　　38　**地下の村 3**　Underground village 3

37　地下の村 2　Underground village 2

● インテリア シリーズ Interior series

39 炉辺談話 Living room
40 キッチン Kitchen
41 インテリア Interior

42　ベッドルーム　Bed room
43　バスルーム　Bath room

●生物シリーズ　Biomorphose series

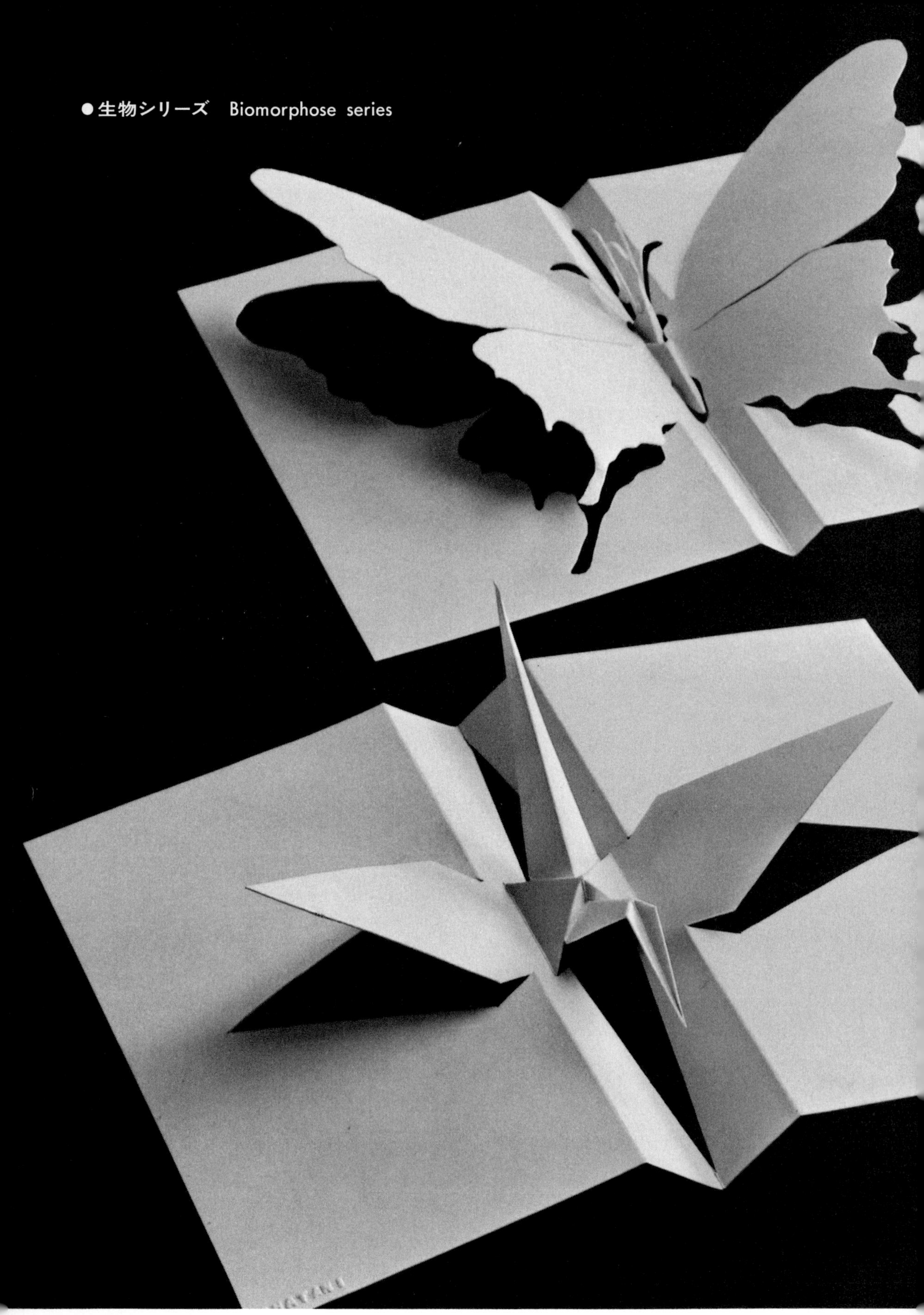

44　蝶　Papillon　　　　45　鶴　Crane

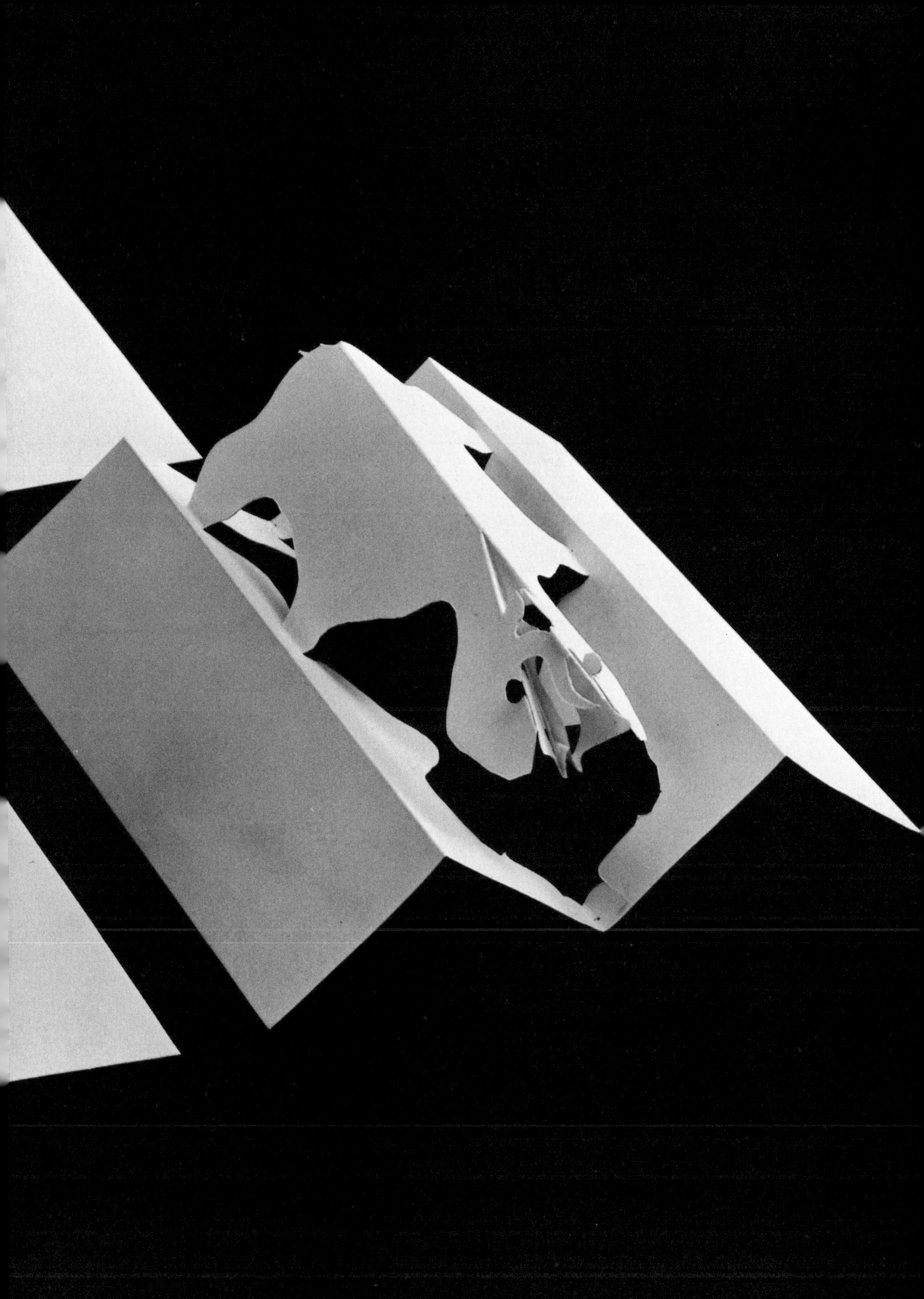

46　丑(牛)　Cattle

47 ORIGAMIC ARCHITECTURE　Origamic Architecture 1

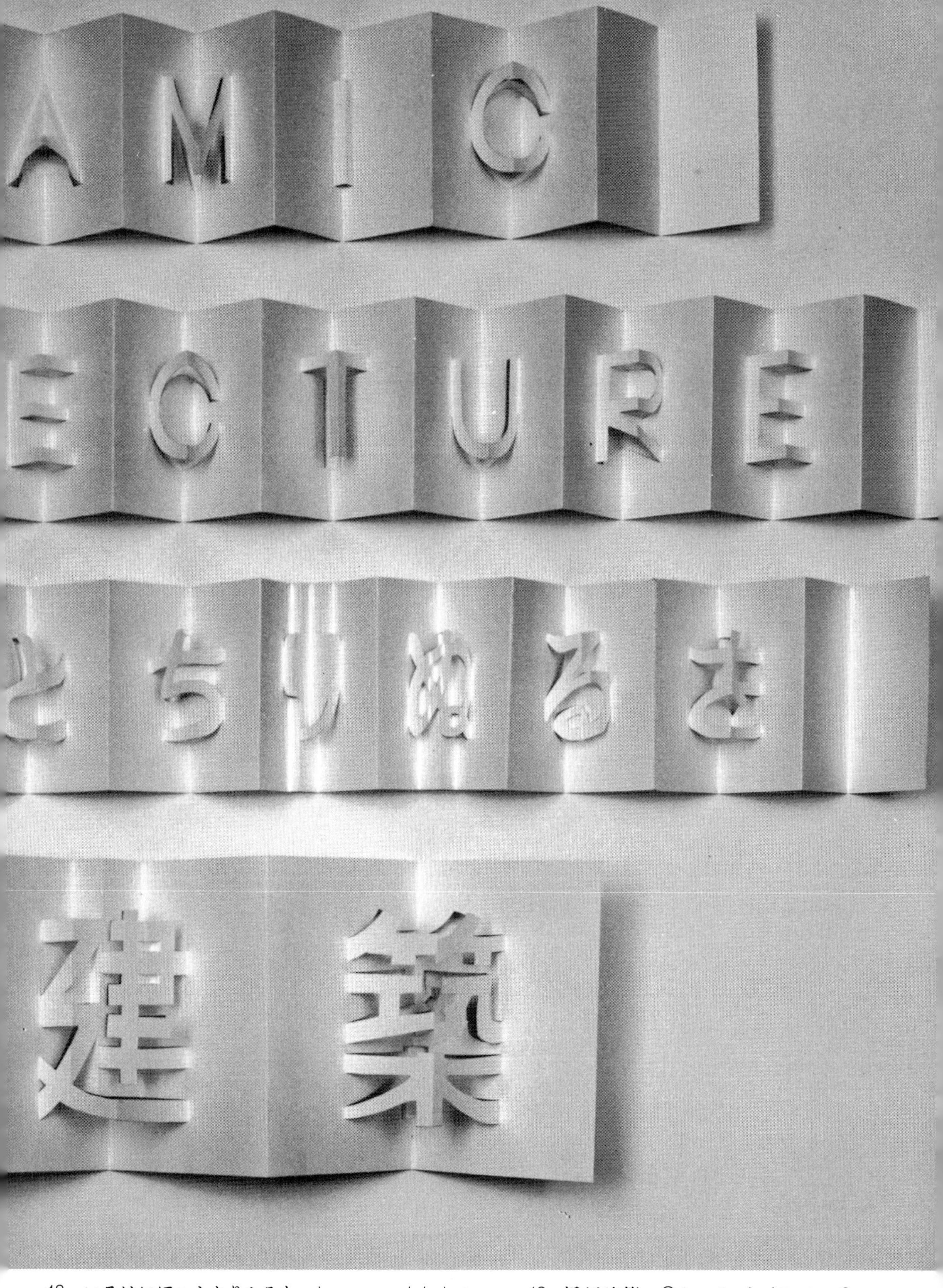

48 いろはにほへとちりぬるを Japanese alphabet　49 折紙建築 Origamic Architecture 2

50 寿 Good luck 1

51 壽 Good luck 2

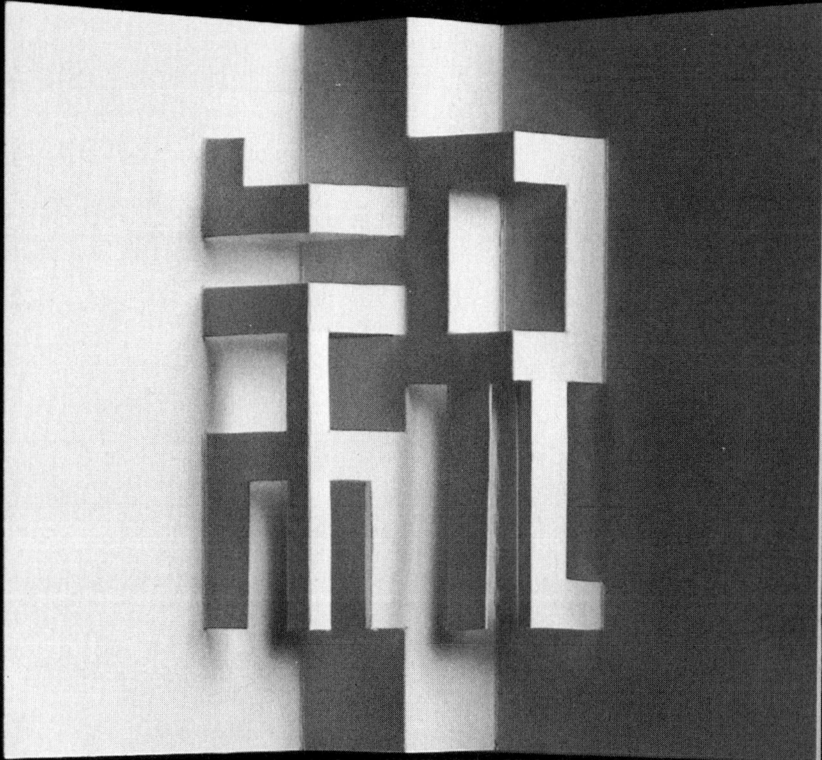

52 祝 Celebration

53 賀 Congratulation

54　シドニーオペラハウス　Sydney opera house

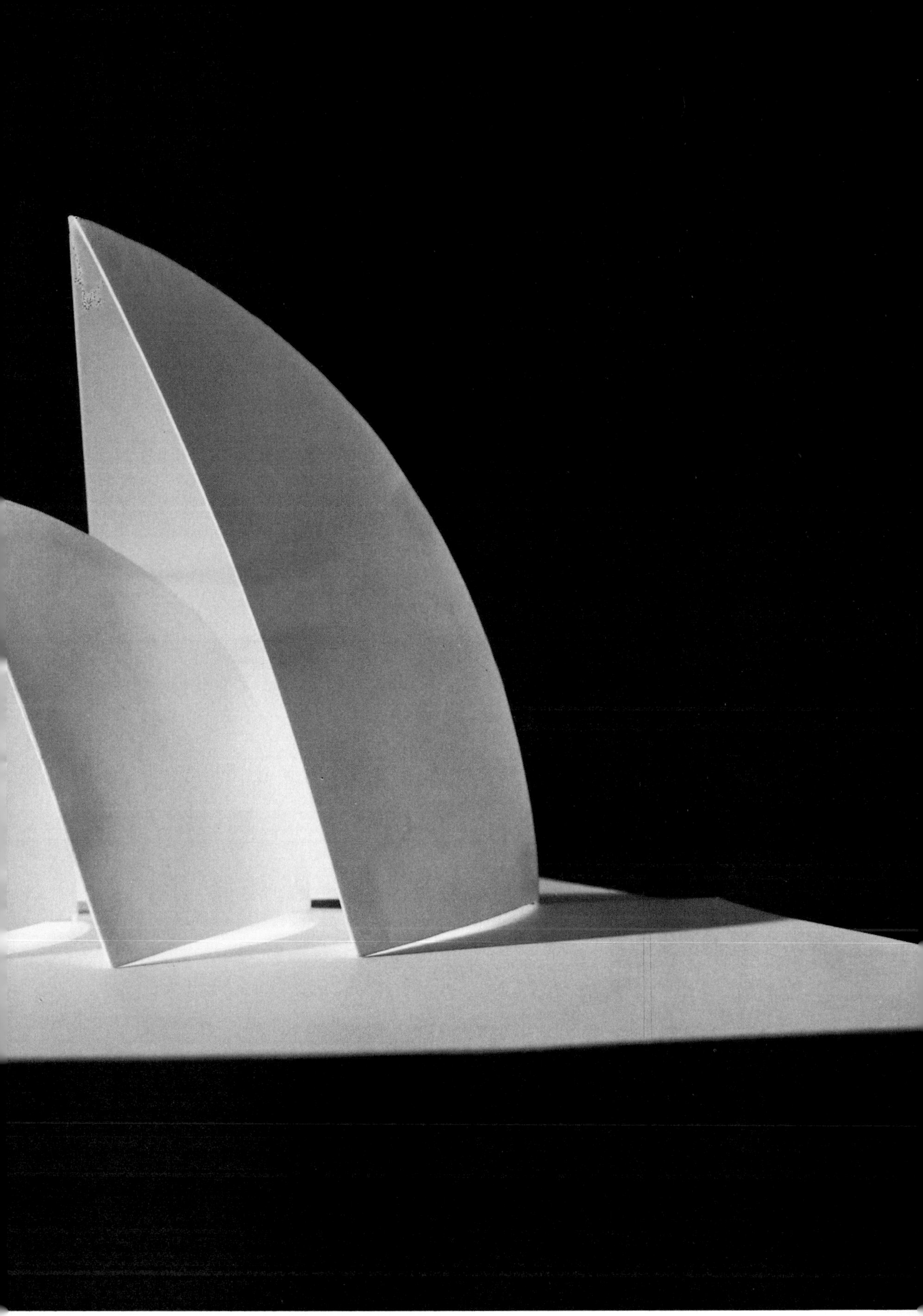

55　ピラミッド1　Pyramid 1　　56　ピラミッド2　Pyramid 2

83　傘堂　Umbrella

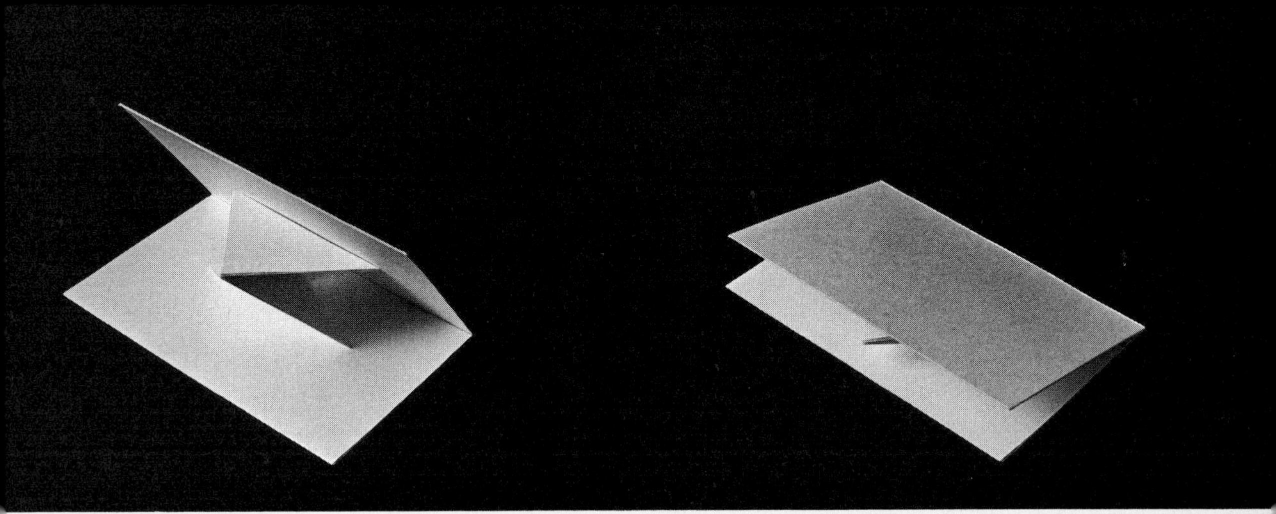

57　精霊の家　Spirit house

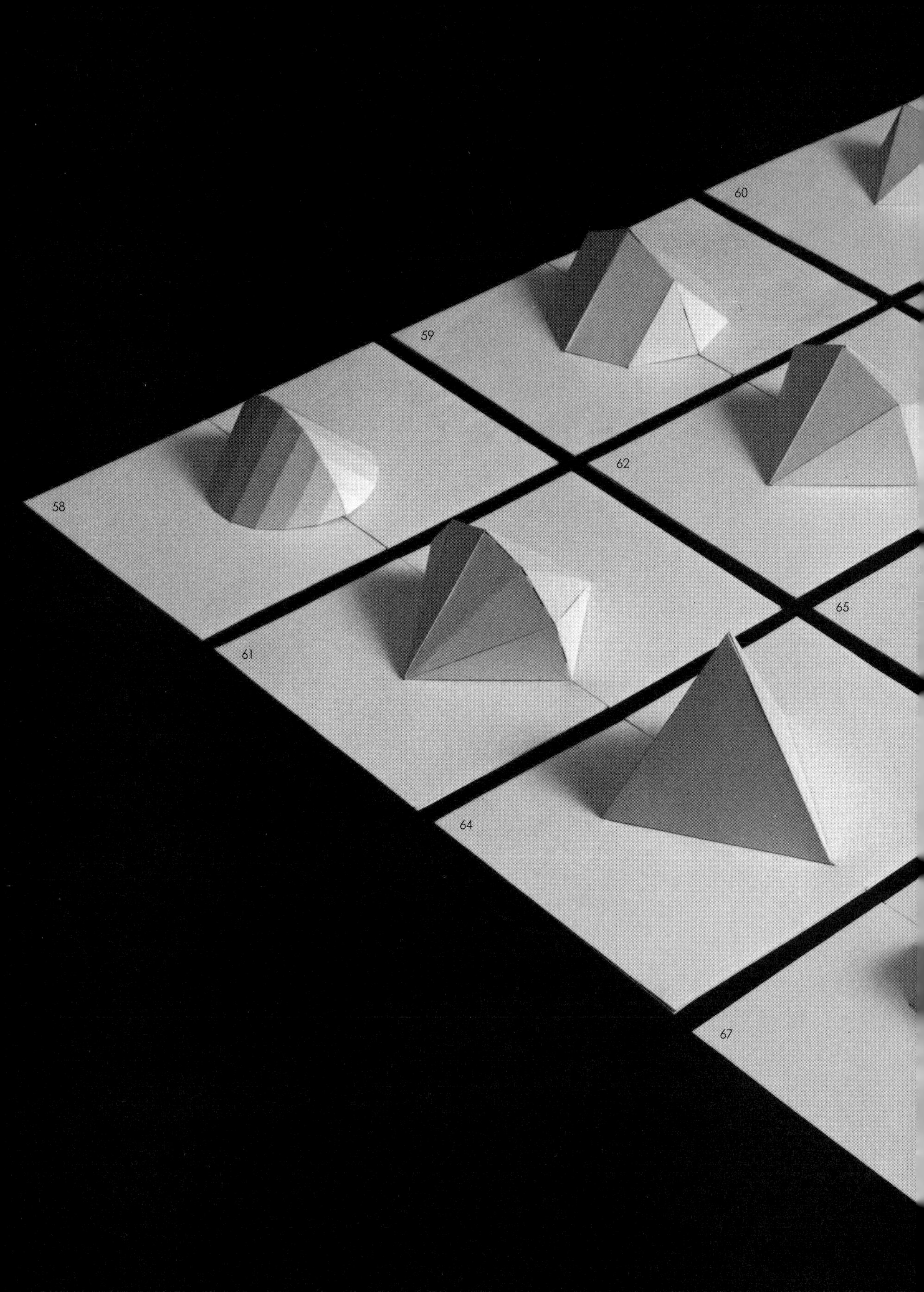

58～63　**半球儀1～6**　Hemisphere 1～6
64　**三角錐**　Tetrahedron
65　**五角錐**　Pentagonal pyramid

66　六角錐 Hexagonal pyramid
67　七角錐 Heptagonal pyramid

70　地球儀　Globe
68　八角錐 Octagonal pyramid

69　円錐 Cone

71　ワールドトレードセンター　New York　　72　ツインタワー　Twin tower
73　尖塔　Trans America　　74　ピサの斜塔　Leaning tower

75　バベルの塔　Tower of Babel
76　ブリッジ　Bridge

77 **凱旋門** L'arc de Triomphe
79 **包** Pao

78 **コートハウス** Courtyard house
80 **ストンヘンジ** Stonehenge

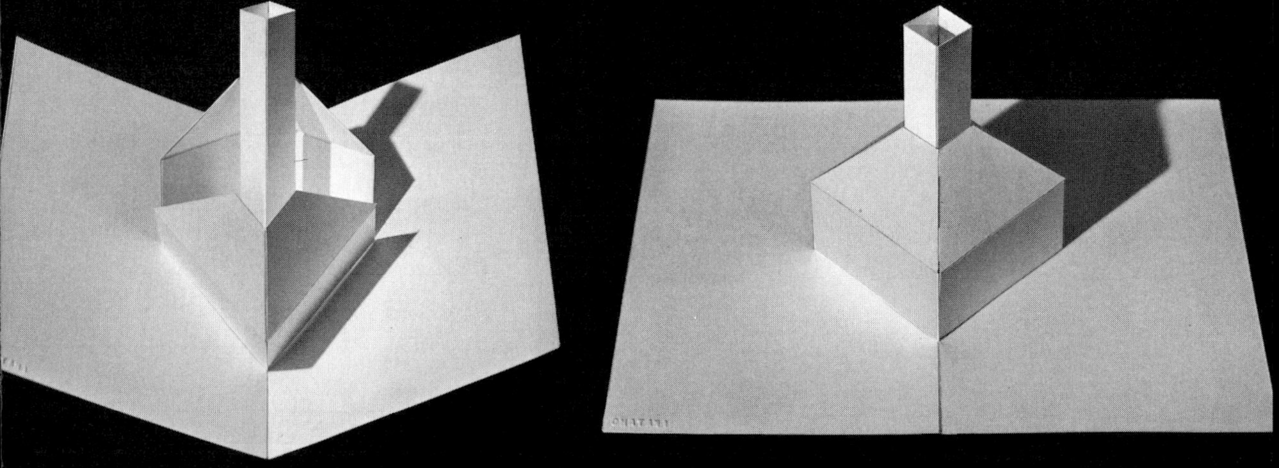

81　サンタクロースの家　Chimney　　　82　銀閣堂　Two storied

● 屋根シリーズ　Roof series

83　傘堂　Umbrella　　84　ヒュッテ　Hütte　　85　方形　Pyramidal

86 寄棟 Hipped roof
87 くど造り Funnel
88 曲り屋 L–shaped
89 切妻 Gabled
90 六角堂 Hexagon
91 入母屋 Hipped gable

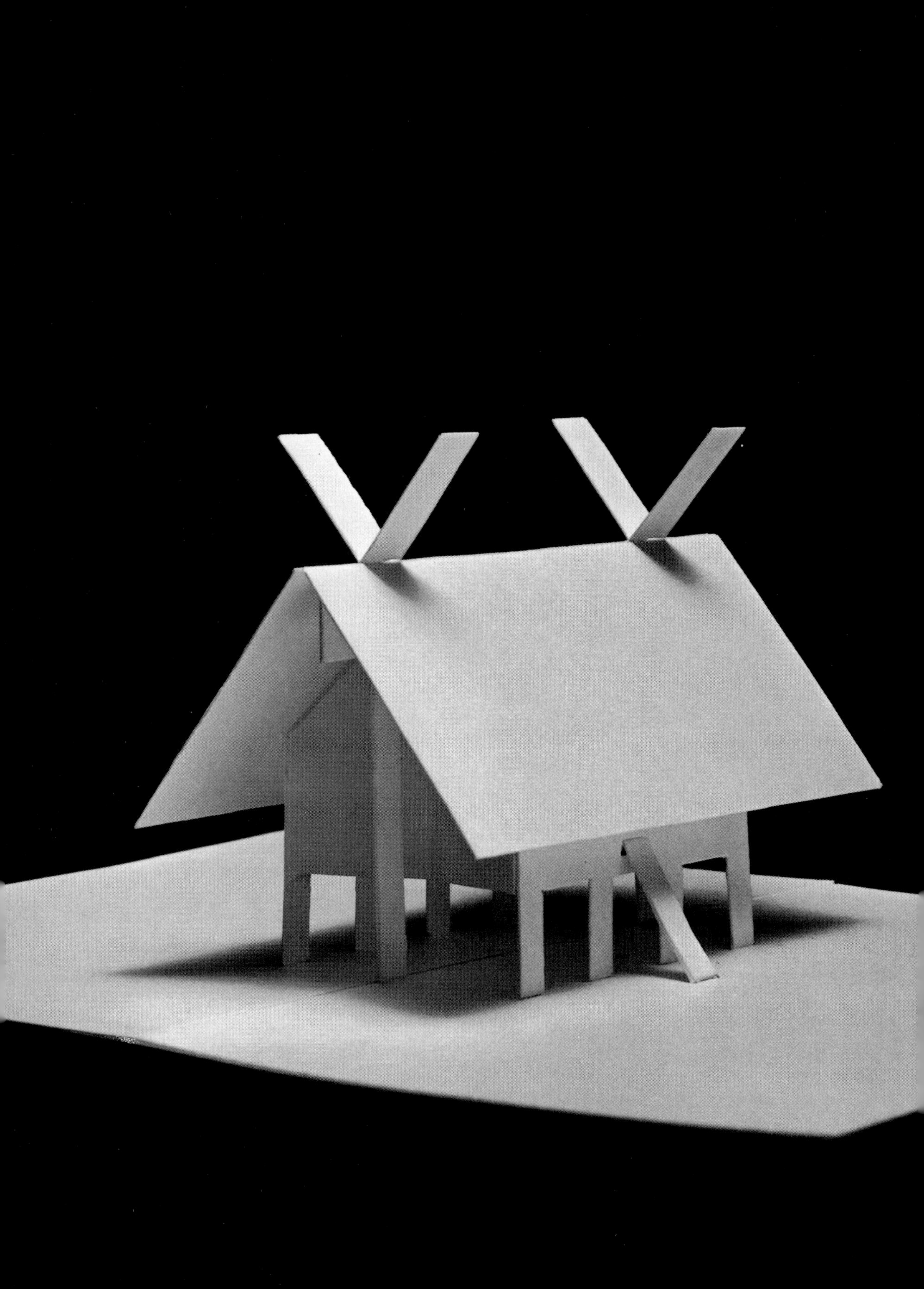

92　お伊勢さん　Ise shrine

93　ペンローズの階段　Penrose stair　　94　ペンローズの三角形　Penrose triangle

●線体シリーズ　Linearoid series

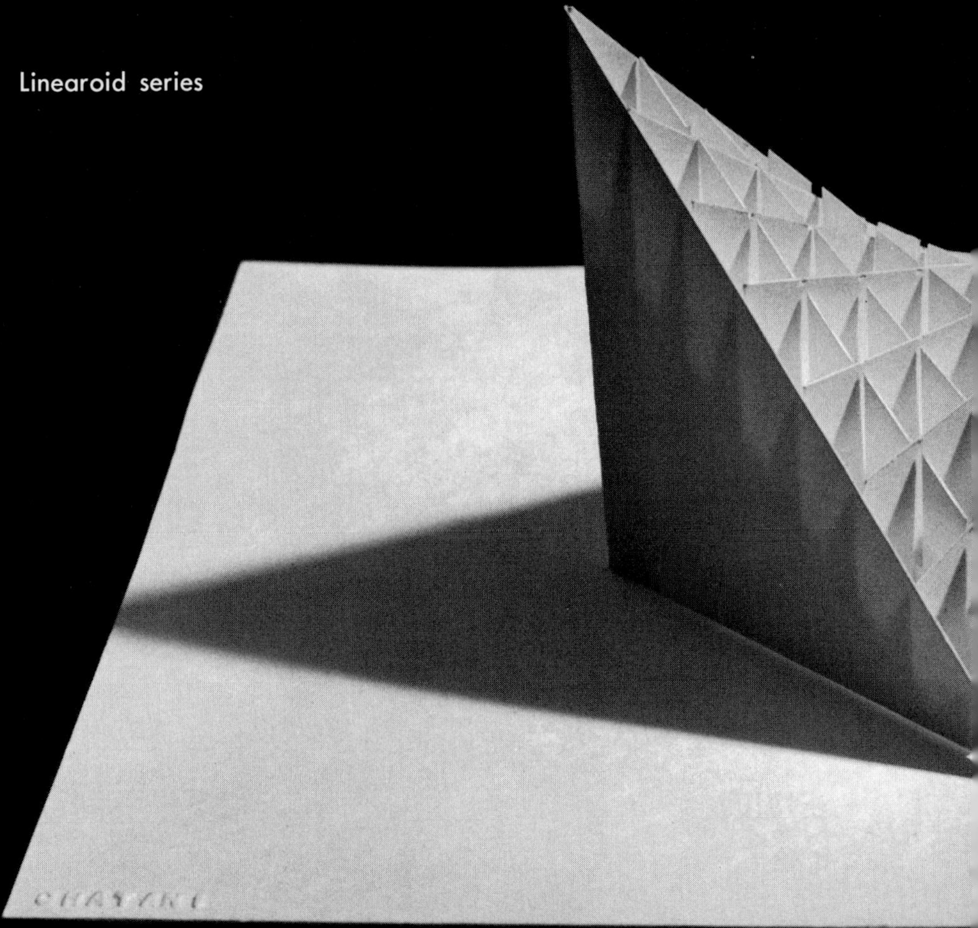

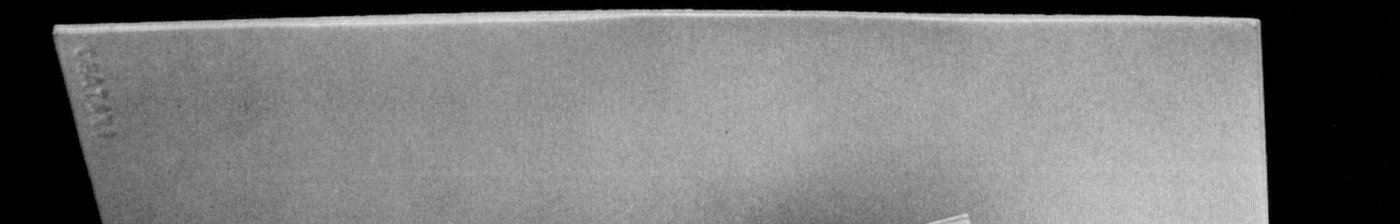

95　H.P.シェル　Hyperbolic Paraboloid 1

95

96　数学者の家　Hyperbolic Paraboloid 2

97　半球　Hemisphere 7

98　球　Sphere

99　スイスの樹　Alpine tree

100　組木　Habitat '84

●完全立体シリーズ　Holohedra series

101　**正八面体**　Octahedron

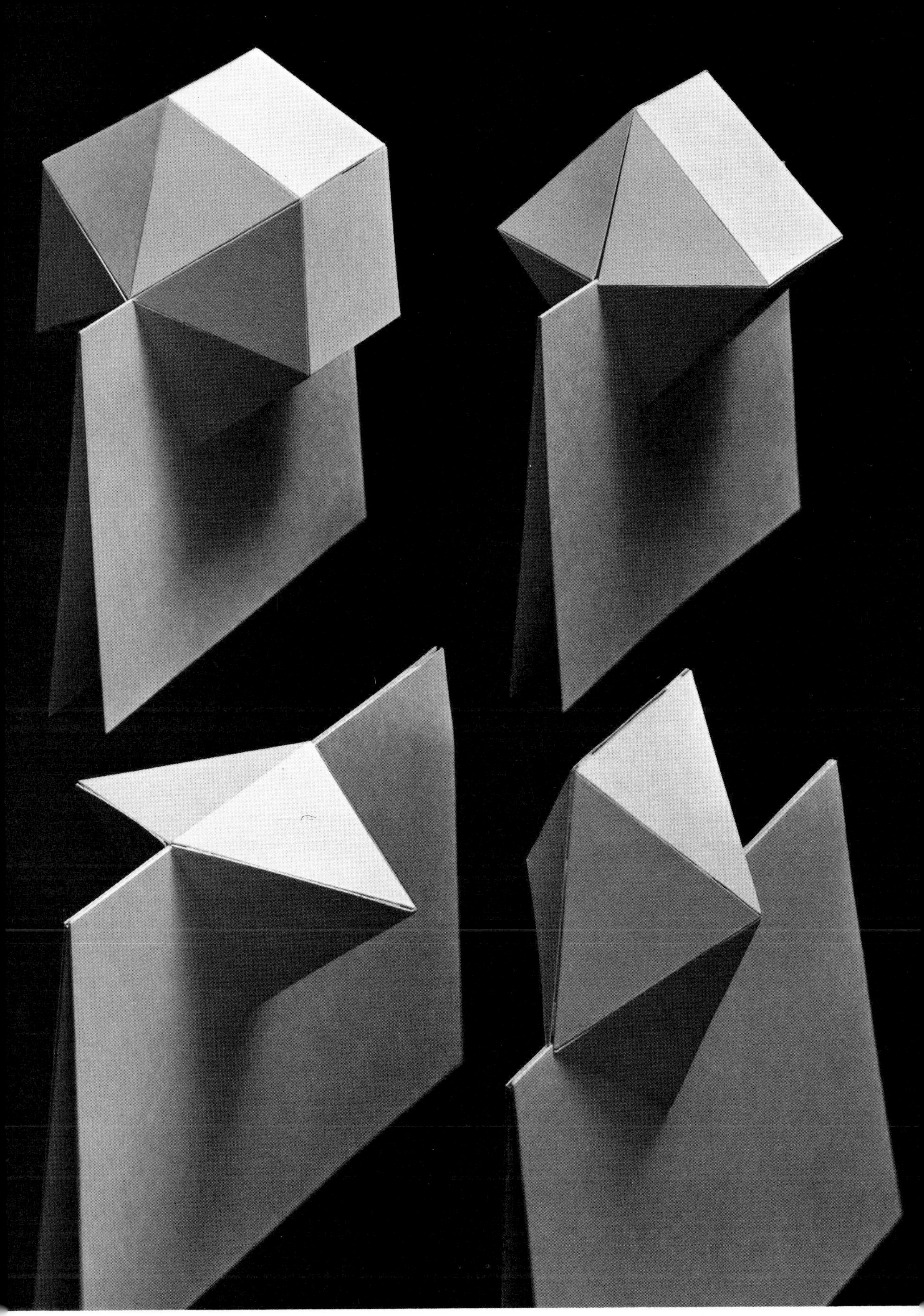

102　**十八面体**　Octadecahedron

103　**十二面体**　Dodecahedron

104　**六面体**　Triangular di-pyramid

105　**十面体**　Pentagonal di-pyramid

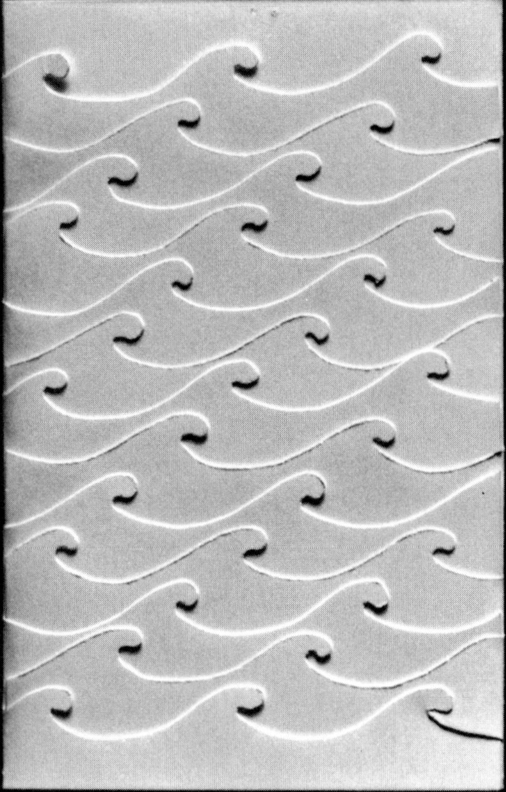

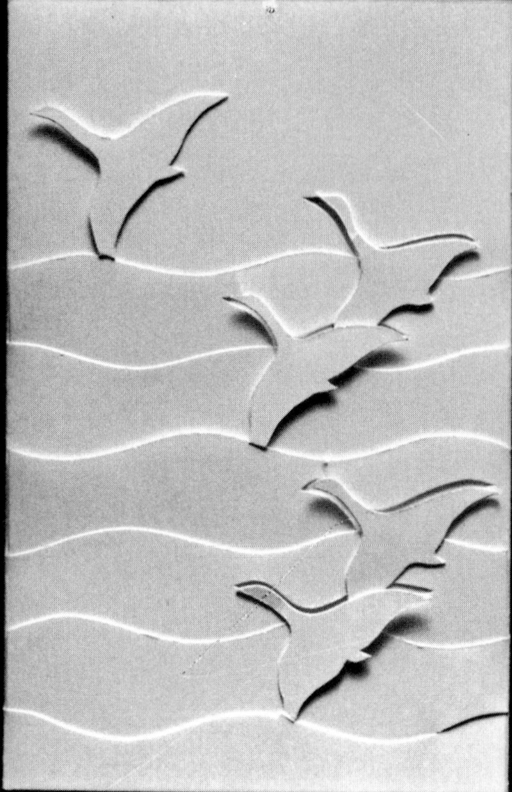

●平面シリーズ
Plain series

106 荒磯 Reefy shore　　107 いそしぎ Flyway

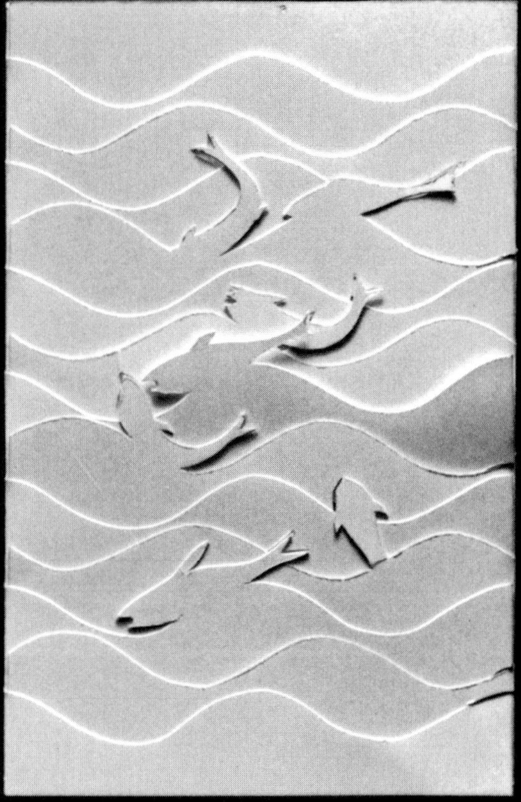

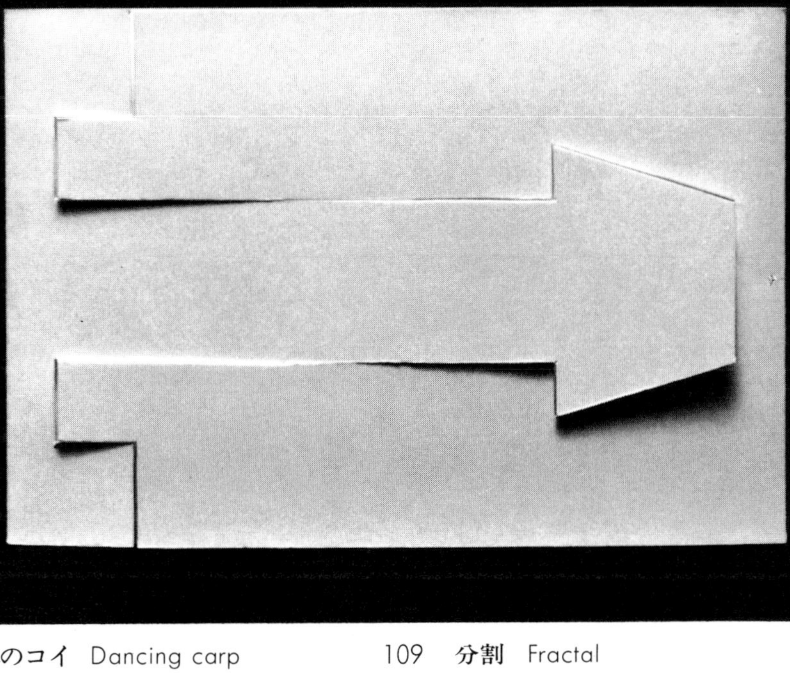

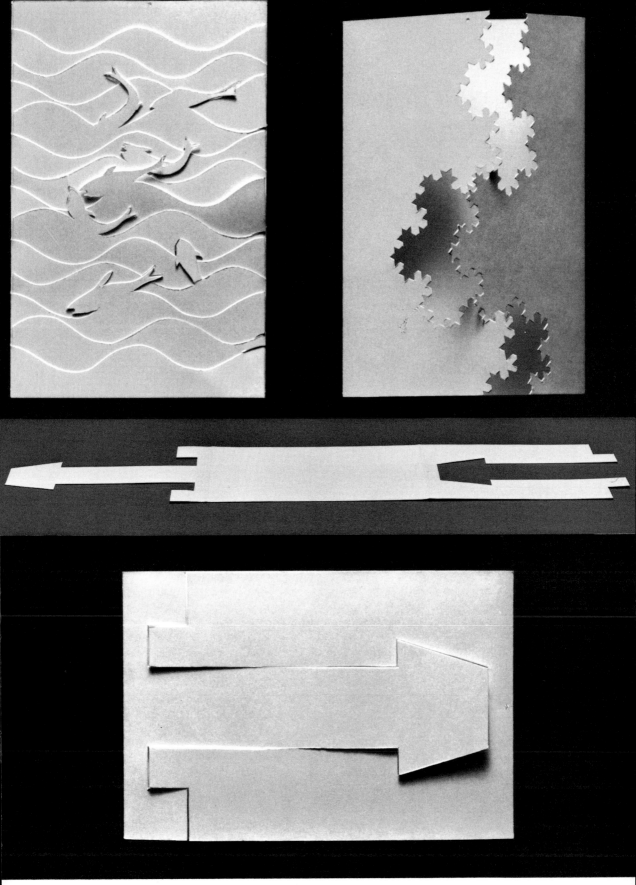

108　たわむれのコイ　Dancing carp　　109　分割　Fractal
110　鎌継　Mortise and tenon joint

111　愛　Love

II Making 作る

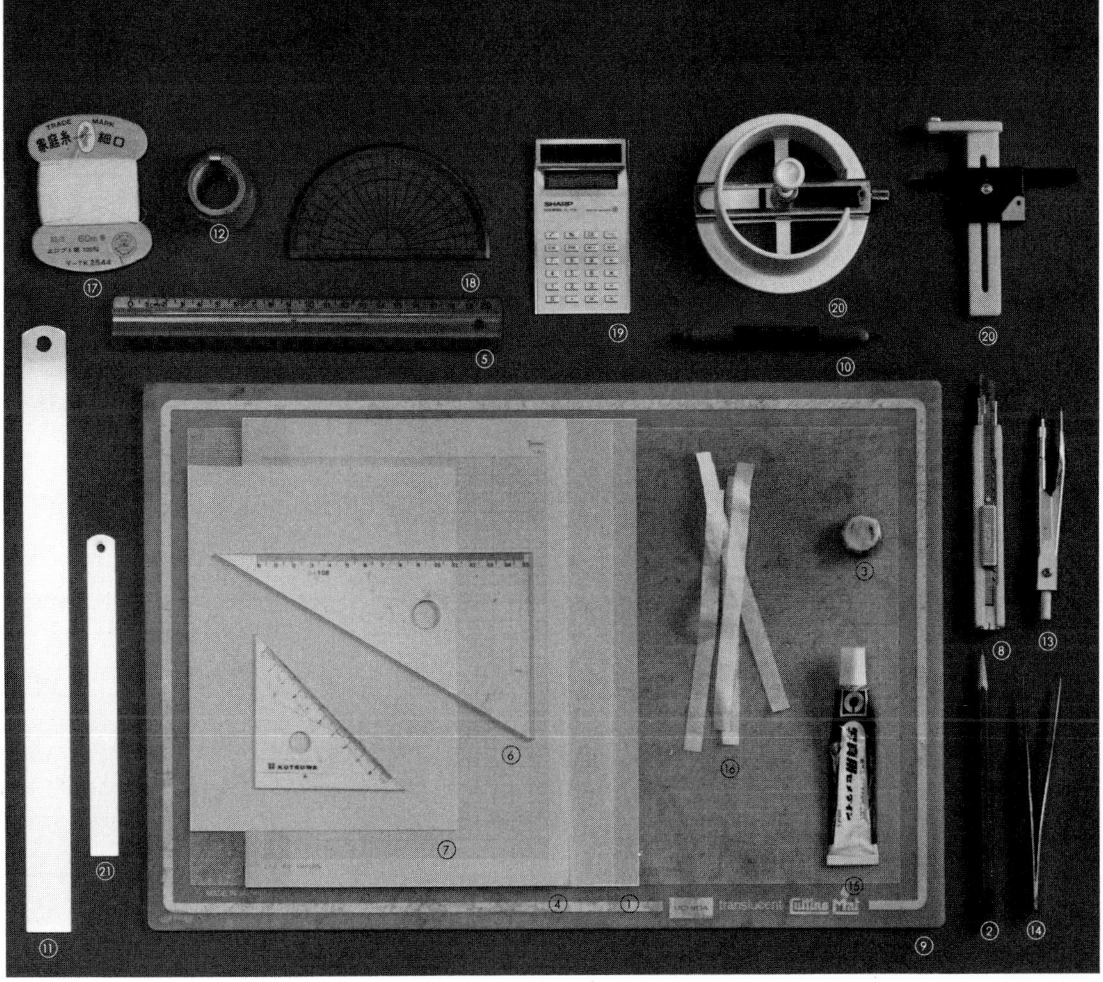

オリガミック・アーキテクチャーの型

[1] 90°に開く型

往復はがき大のケント紙に，切れ目と折り目を入れ，二つ折りにすると出来上がり。90°に開くと立体が現れ，180°まで開くと元の1枚の紙に戻るという，それだけ。それだけに，さまざまの形が簡単に現れる不思議さと清楚な意匠を楽しめます。

[2] 90°の型を背中合わせにしたもの

90°に開く型を2枚作って背中合わせにしたり，1枚つづきにつなげて作ると，一見180°に開く型のよう，別名180°風です。背中合わせの面を写真糊ではると完成。さらに，4枚つなぎにすれば，一見360°風となり，いずれも折りたたんで，はがき大です。

[3] 180°に開く型

90°に開く型を作ってから，本格的な，180°の型に進みます。

二つ折りの紙からどんな立体が飛び出すのか見当がつかず，180°に開く途中も，作為を越えた不思議な動きを示します。この楽しみはぜひとも実物を開いて味わって下さい。

[4] 360°に開く型

立体をたためないか，日本古来の「たとう」をいたずらした果てのオリジナル。いま5種類，作り方は180°に開く型と全く同じです。

[5] 0°のままの型

十二単のように重なったり，つながらないように見えて，実は1枚の紙なのがミソ。90°から360°まで開く型を考えた末に生まれた，立体感の思い入れ。

材料と道具

①スケッチ用紙，②鉛筆，③消しゴム，④設計(型紙)用方眼紙(セクションペーパー 1㎜目，B5サイズ)，⑤物指，⑥三角定規，⑦ケント紙か画用紙，⑧カッターナイフ，⑨下敷（カッティングマットか厚紙)，⑩細い鉄筆と太い鉄筆，⑪スチール物指，⑫セロテープ，⑬コンパス，⑭先のとがったピンセット，⑮写真糊，⑯和紙，⑰白木綿糸，⑱分度器，⑲電卓，⑳円カッター，㉑薄鉄板

（63ページ参照）

90°に開く型を基本として①～⑫，特殊な場合に①～⑮，180°と360°の型では①～⑰，特殊な場合に①～⑳，0°の型では①～⑫と㉑を用い，大体は普通の文房具店でそろいます。

道具は，できるだけ簡素にし，必要に応じてそろえること。使うのは頭と手なのです。

設計

まず，作りたい立体の図形をスケッチして見当をつけます。次は設計製図，輪郭と二つ折りの基本線から始めます。

90°に開く型の場合，切れ目(実線——) と山折り(点線……)，谷折り(鎖線- - -) を書いていきます。

折り目が，山折りか谷折りか分かりにくいときは，点線で書いておき，後から鎖線にします。

折り目の位置を確かめるのに，74ページの図に示す2種の断面が役立ちます。一つは方眼紙のます目に対角線で書くため，実際より大きく($\sqrt{2}$ ≒1.4倍)なりますが，簡便です。

図形の安定感や比率などを練り，試作で確かめていきます。

180°と360°に開く型の場合，立面図と，たたんだ図が混乱しないように製図します。たたんだ図は，はみ出さないぎりぎりの大きさが効果的です。立体各面の寸法は電卓で計算します。

台紙

建築でいえば敷地に相当する台紙は，90°に開く型の場合，ケント紙をほぼ往復はがきの大きさ(15cm×20cm)に切ります。14 簾，24 ポストモダン，27 円型劇場，36～38 地下の村，は特殊な寸法ですが，いずれも，たたむとはがき大になります。

47と48の文字は，10cm角が1文字分です。

180°と360°の型では，はがき大の大きさ(10cm×15cm)を和紙で2枚つなぎにして台紙とします。0°の型は，10cmか15cmの幅で，出来上がりははがき大とします。好きな大きさで作ってもかまいません。

製作

90°に開く型は，まず，設計図(型紙)の輪郭線を山折りし(裏側に折り)，ケント紙の台紙にかぶせます。次に，下敷の上で，折り目と切れ目の位置を，細い鉄筆で突いて下のケント紙に写します。印は，大きい方がはっきり分かり，出来上がると気になりません。

かぶせた型紙をはずし，台紙を下敷にのせ，太い鉄筆で印をつなげながら，折り目をつけていきます。山折りの折り目は，裏側からつける方がきれいに折れますが，型紙との対応が難しいときは，こだわらないことにします。

折り目の次に切れ目を入れます。曲線など，スチール物指に頼らないで切っていくときも，ゆっくり少しずつ。刃物などで指や机やケント紙を傷めないよう気をつけて下さい。

いよいよ折り方。端の方，大きい折り目から，両手の指を表裏全体にかけ，だましだまし折り目を強めていきます。

試作は，本当はまだ設計中の段階というべきでしょう。手直しの末に，うまくいったとき，小さな小さな建築を作った大きな喜びにひたることができます。

180°～360°シリーズの場合

型紙の中には，平面図，立面図，折りたたんだ状態の展開図，実寸法の求め方などが描かれています。図を読み分け，太線の展開図に沿って，部品を必要な数だけつくり，完成図形と折りたたみ図形の両方を勘案しながらつないで，次第に形を整えていきます。

整った形の示す緊張感と折りたたむときの形の変化の意外さは見事なものです。

180°に開く型は，まず，ケント紙の端切れを，計画している立体の各面に切り抜き，和紙片を張ってうまくつなぎ，台紙に固定すべき点に糸をつけます。たたんだり開いたり具合を見てから，鉄筆で台紙に穴をあけ，ピンセットで糸を通し，裏で留めて具合を調整します。成功したあなたはオリガミック・アーキテクト，折り紙付きの建築家！

0°のうち，109，110，111は，台紙の中央に薄鉄板をのせ，左右の端を上に折り重ねて，カッターで切ります。2枚重ねを同時に切らねばなりません。

90°と0°の型は量産が容易です。

さらに，大きさ・材質・色彩・動きの工夫を目指してはいかが？

裏打ち

90°に開く型のうち，19 パルテノン，30 崖の家などは，台紙と同寸法のケント紙を，写真糊で裏打ちする必要があります。糊はこまめに蓋をすること。しかし，11 マヤの階段，26 ウェディングパレスなど，裏打ちせず，裏から見る方がきれい（バックシャン）です。

180°と360°に開く型は，糸でかがった裏を台紙補強を兼ねて，裏打ちします。なお，立体の各面も，それぞれ1㎜ずつ小さい図形を切って裏打ちすると，糸のかがりがかくれ，縁の厚みが増して，出来上がりが際立ってきます。

180°シリーズ　制作写真説明

180° type. Process of assembly with photographs

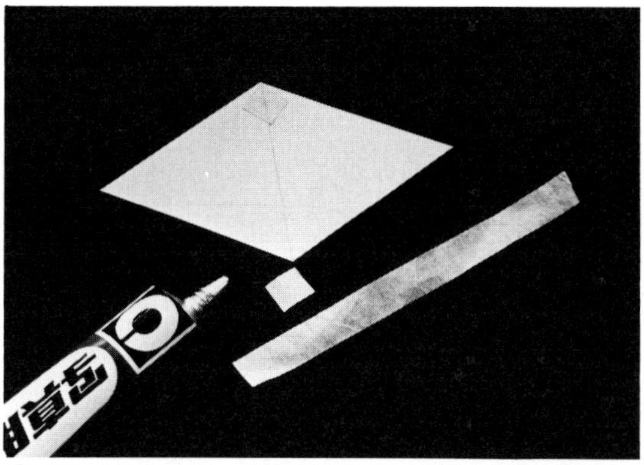

①立体の組み立て：和紙にのりをつけて，立体部品のケント紙の裏をはりつなぐ。

Assembling the cube : Join the parts together with small pieces of Japanese paper (*Washi*) glued to the back of each component.

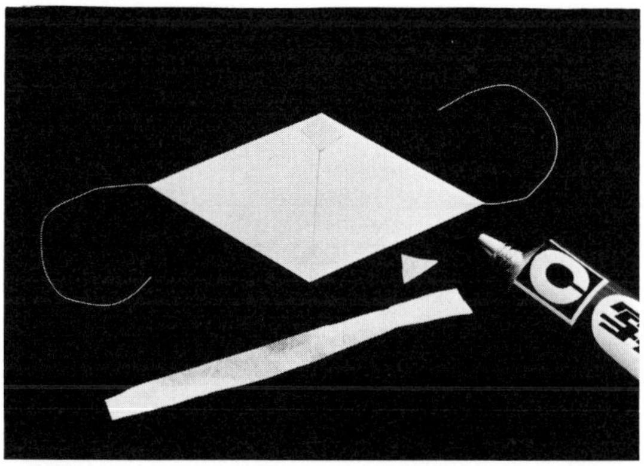

②台紙にかがる糸のつけ方：立体部品のケント紙の裏の隅にのりをつけ，糸を指で押さえてはりつけ，その上をさらに，のりをつけた和紙片ではる。

How to join the object to the base paper : Glue the thread to the corner of the reverse side of the Kent paper and cover with small pieces of *Washi*.

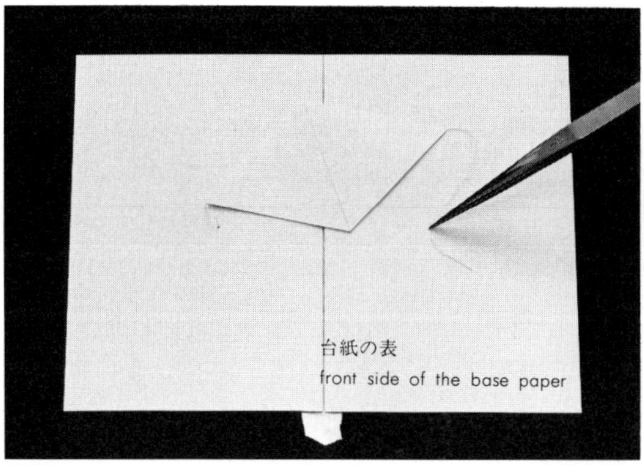

③ピンセットの先で糸をつかみ，台紙の穴に通す。

Pull the thread through the hole in the base paper with pointed pincers.

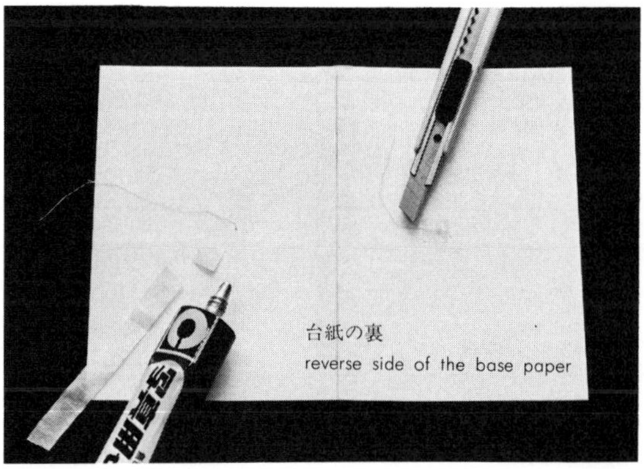

④裏に通した糸を引っ張って，のりで台紙に指で押さえてはり，その上をさらにのりをつけた和紙片ではる。余った糸はカッターで切る。

Pull the thread through the hole, stick it to the reverse side of the base paper, cover these points with small pieces of *Washi* , and cut off the excess thread.

Types of Origamic Architecture

[1] The 90° open type

Take a double Kent paper postcard, cut along cutting lines and score folding lines. Open 90° and a form appears. If opened 180° the card reverts to flatness. This example is very simple but many magical and mysterious forms can be made to appear by simple cutting and folding.

[2] The Back to back 90° open type

Take two double postcards, fold in the middle and glue back to back. At first glance it looks like an open 180° type. Take two more cards, glue together and affix to the first so that the entire object looks like a 360° open type. If folded flat it reverts to a single postcard size.

[3] The 180° open type

Having successfully completed the 90° type you can proceed a step further to the 180° type.

It is difficult to imagine what shapes you can make appear from two sheets of paper but the gradual and sequential appearance of form is particularly enjoyable in this type.

[4] The 360° open type

I developed the 360° open type having first studied the properties of the flattened cube and Japanese traditional toys. The method of making it is the same as that of the 180° type.

[5] The 0° type

Although the 0° type appears to be made of layers of paper, it is actualy made of a single sheet. This is the final type in the 90°, 180° and 360° series and although it is not a cube, it invokes the same effect.

Materials and Tools

① Sketch pad ② Pencil ③ Eraser
④ Graph paper ⑤ Scale ⑥ Set square
⑦ White Kent paper ⑧ Cutting knife
⑨ Cutting board ⑩ Thick and thin stylus pen
⑪ Steel ruler ⑫ Clear adhesive tape
⑬ Compasses ⑭ Pointed pincers
⑮ Photographic paste
⑯ Japanese paper (washi)
⑰ White cotton thread ⑱ Protractor
⑲ Calculator ⑳ Circle cutter
㉑ Small steel cutting plate
(Shown in p.63)

Depending on the type which you wish to make, the required materials are different. For 90° types, materials ①—⑫ are required and in special cases ①—⑮. For 180° and 360° types ①—⑰ and in special cases ①—⑳. For 0° types ①—⑫ and ㉑. All materials should be available at normal stationary shops.

Design

Firstly, sketch the shape or form which you wish to produce. Next, draw the cutting and folding lines on the pattern sheet.

If you are making a 90° type, mark the cutting line thus ———, the ridge fold line thus ·········, and the valley fold line thus ---------. It is useful to refer to the two sections (Shown on page 74) to clarify the positions of the cutting and folding lines. Both of them are shown on the pattern sheet.

Using the diagonal lines on the graph paper, the simulated form will appear bigger than the real one. Stability and proportion are both established through trial and error. In the cases of both the 180° and 360° open types you should be careful not to confuse the 'open' and 'folded' positions when you draw them. Try to avoid making the folded shape too small. Preferably make the edges of the desired form as close to the edges of the post card as possible. To be exact, the areas of each surface should be ascertained using a calculator.

Base paper

If this were real architecture, the base paper would be the site. For 90° types the base paper is 15cms × 20cms. No.14 (screen) No.24 (post modern) No.27 (Amphitheatre) and No's 36, 37 and 38 (Underground village) are exceptional sizes. If folded however, they would revert to the same size. No's 41, 47 and 48 are each 10cms × 10cms. In the case of the 180° and 360° types, the base paper is 10cms × 15cms and consists of two postcards joined together with a thin strip of Japanese paper (Washi). For the 0° type, a width of 10cms or 15cms is preferable. When folded this should become the size of a postcard.

Practical application

The 90° type Take a pattern sheet, fold along the border lines and place over the base paper. With a thin stylus pen dot along both folding and cutting lines. Be sure that the dots leave a clear impression on the base paper.

Remove the pattern sheet and join the dots together. Using a thick stylus pen, score along the folding lines bearing in mind that it is better to score the ridge folds on the back of the paper.

On the cutting lines, cut slowly and be especialy careful when not using a steel ruler. Fold the biggest lines first, press folding using your fingertips. Then, using both hands, gradualy complete the fold. If you find that something goes wrong, do it again. To complete the object is like making mini architecture and is a great pleasure.

180° and 360° open types. The following data is provided on the pattern sheets. Plan, elevation, development of folded forms and how to measure the forms. By carefully looking at the pattern sheets and photographs the necessary number of component parts can be produced. The individual components should be joined together with small pieces of Washi to produce the desired object.

It is very exciting to observe the form being gradually brought to perfection.

Select the points where the object will be joined to the base paper, pierce with a stylus pen and, using pointed pincers, pull the thread through the hole. If you are successful in this delicate task then you are certainly a talented architect !

The 0° type. Take the base paper and put the thin steel cutting plate in the middle. Fold both sides over the steel plate and carefully cut along cutting lines.

In the case of the 90° and 0° types, it is possible to produce many different shapes quite easily. The 180° type is considerably more difficult however, so the numbers of objects which can be produced is limited. Of course, a variety of images can be produced using different sized and coloured paper.

Lining the base for reinforcement

In some of the 90° types, for example No.19 (Parthenon) and No.30 (Cliff house) it is necessary to reinforce the Kent base paper with another sheet or the same size stuck to the back of it with photographic glue. In No.11 (Mayan pyramid) and No.26 (Wedding palace) it is better not to reinforce the base paper as the rear is just as interesting as the frontal view.

In the 180° and 360° types the component parts themselves can be reinforced with slightly smaller pieces of Kent paper which also make the object appear firmer and smarter.

III Drawing 描く

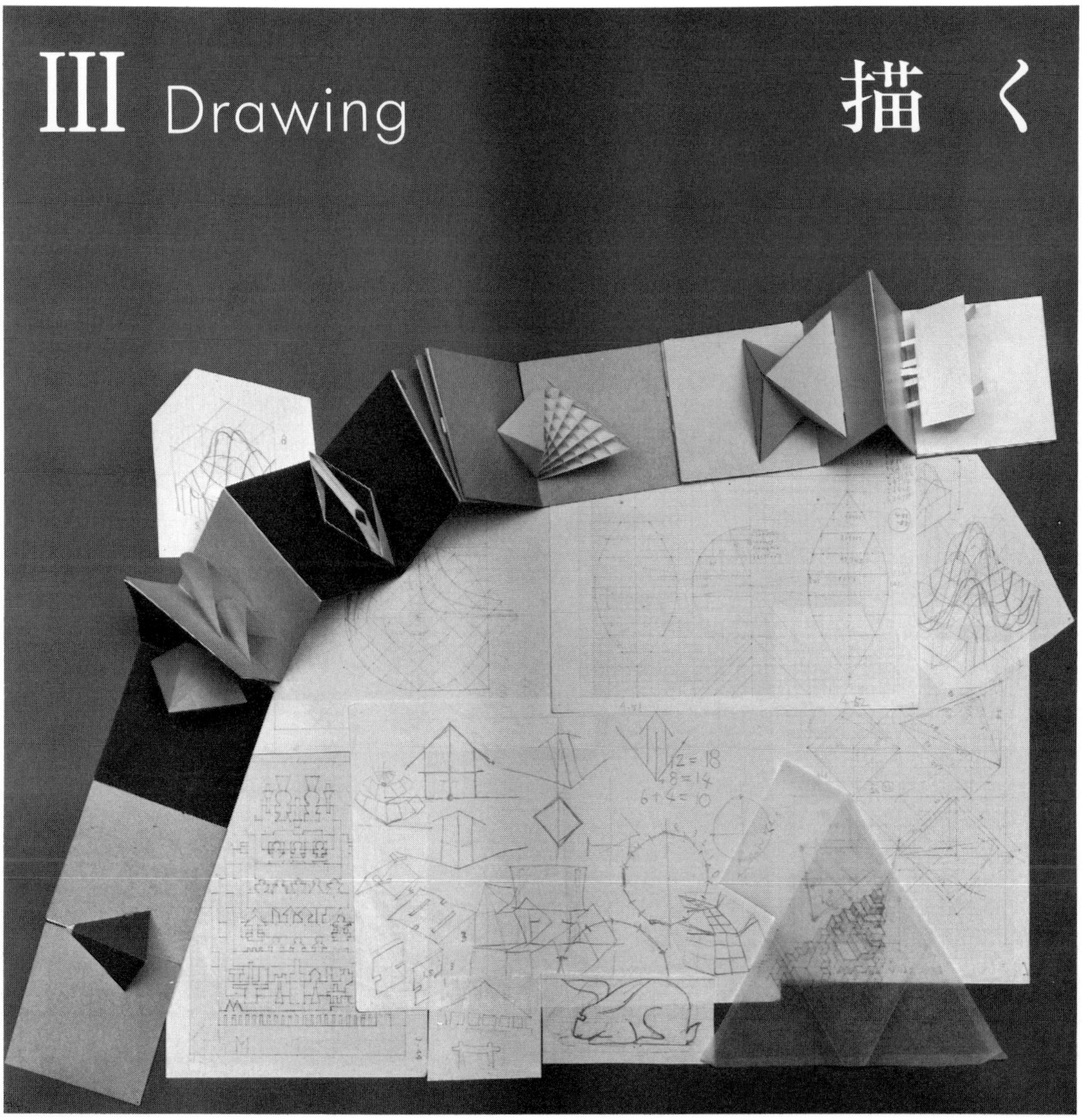

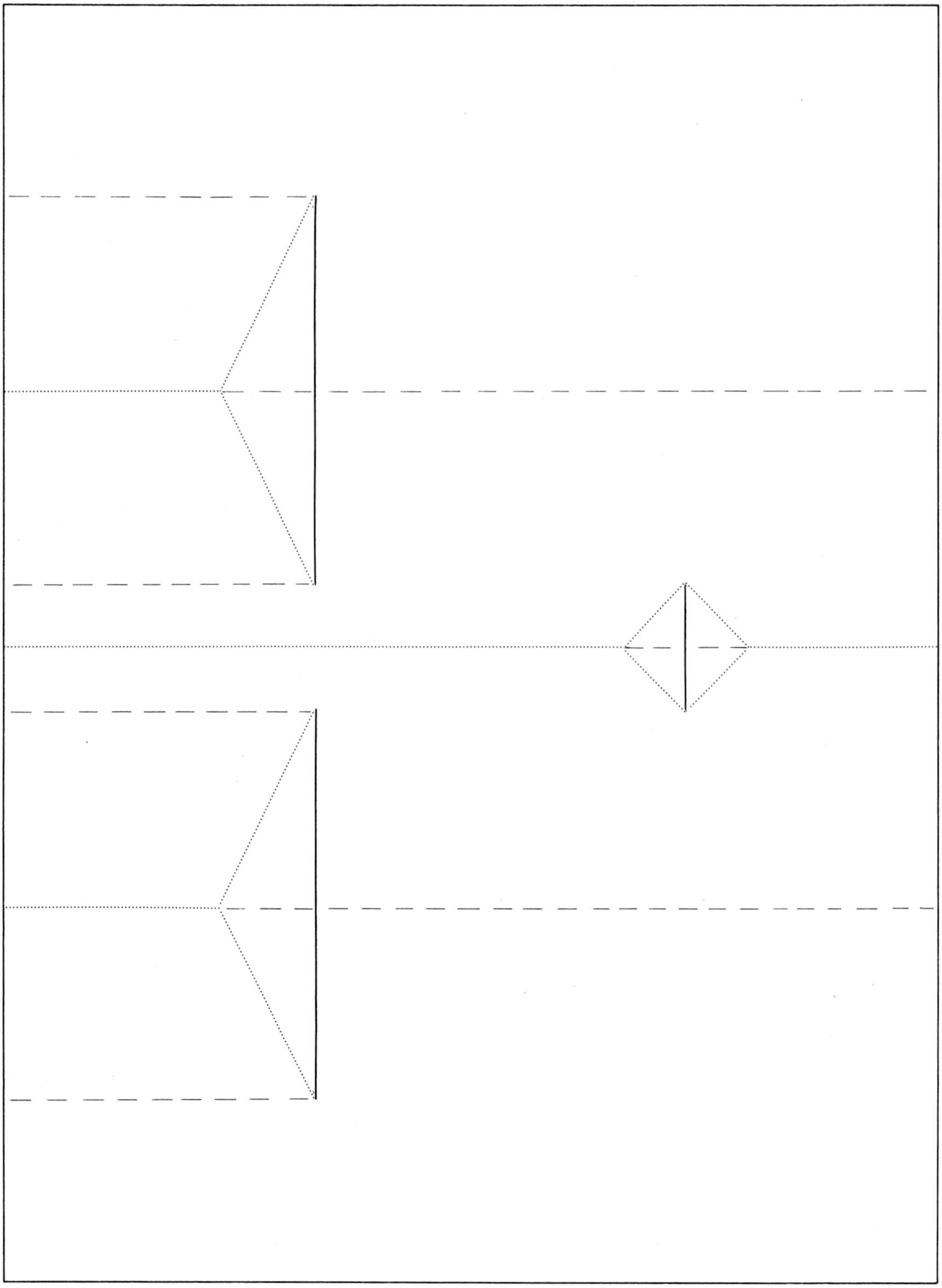

●面シリーズ　Mask series

1　喜　Happiness (1/1)　(　) は縮尺 scale

······山折り線　Ridge fold line
－－－谷折り線　Valley fold line
——切り線（展開図の線）　Cutting line
——平面図の線　Line of plan

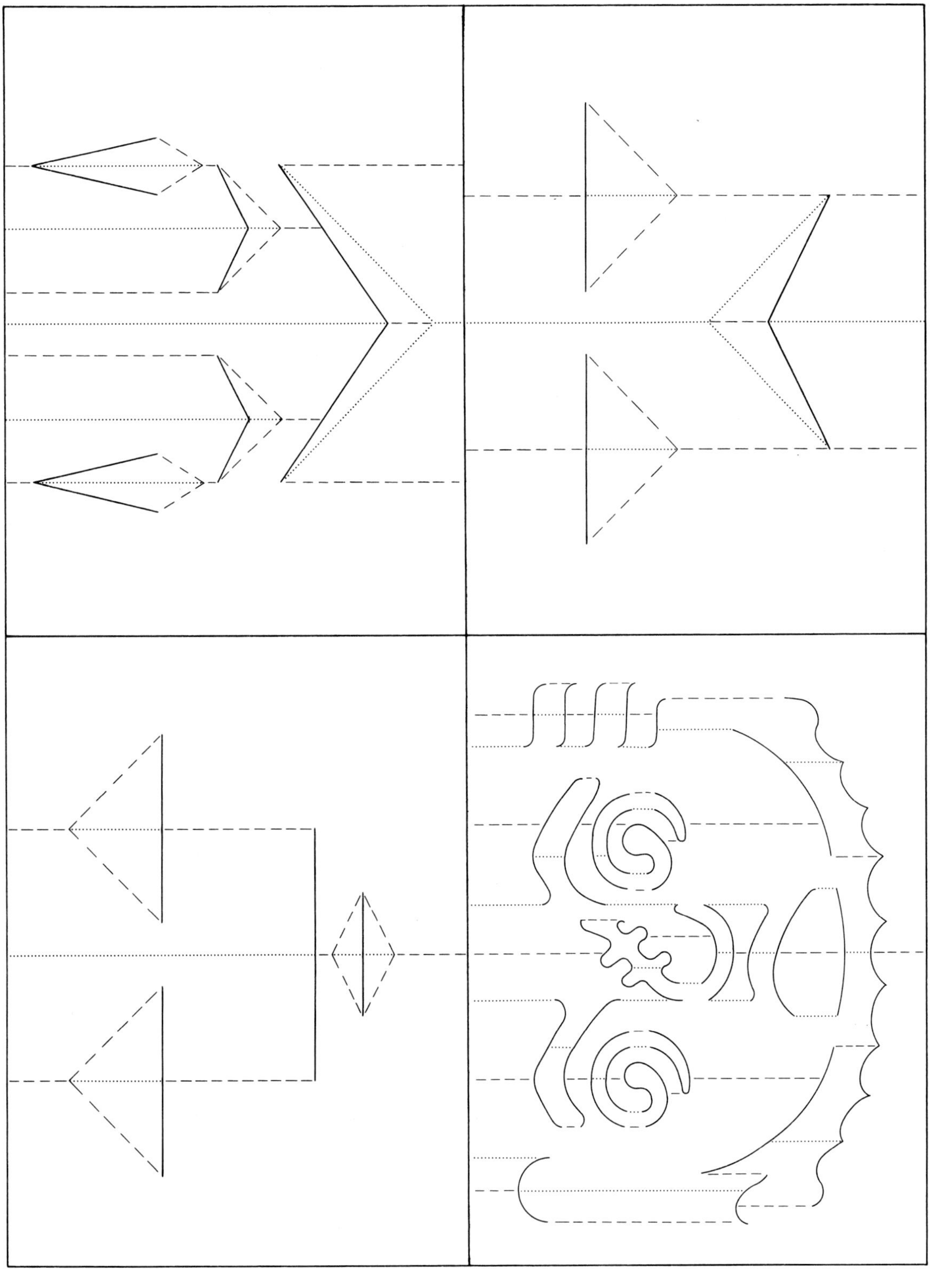

2 怒 Anger (1/2)

3 哀 Grief (1/2)

4 楽 pleasure (1/2)

5 へのへのもへじ Letraface (1/2)

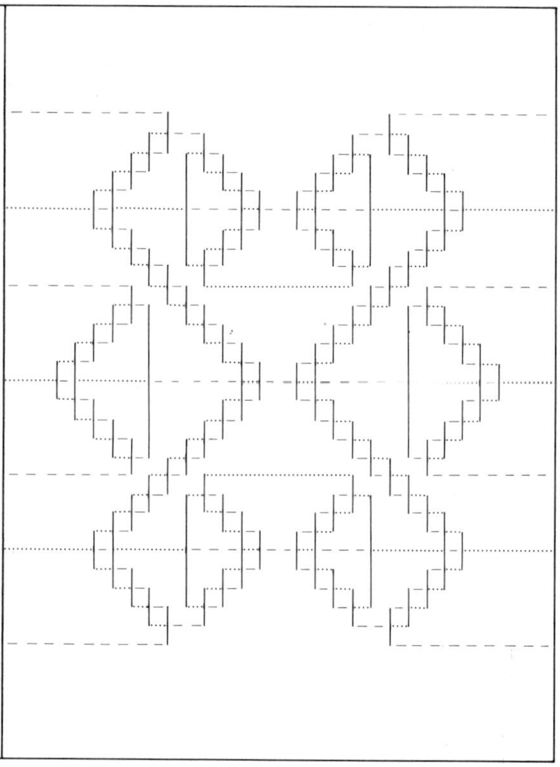

エッシャー讃

エッシャー（オランダ，1898～1972）は，実際にありえない立体図形を2次元のだまし絵に描いたり，魔術師的な不条理の世界を見せてくれます。ペンローズの不可能な三角形や無限階段がモチーフになっています。このような視覚の遊びに挑戦してみたのが，6，7エッシャーの階段と，93ペンローズの階段，94ペンローズの三角形です。

Some of Escher's magic works are based on Penrose's idea of the impossible tribar and stairway. No.'s 6,7,and No.93 are such stairways, while No.94 tribar.

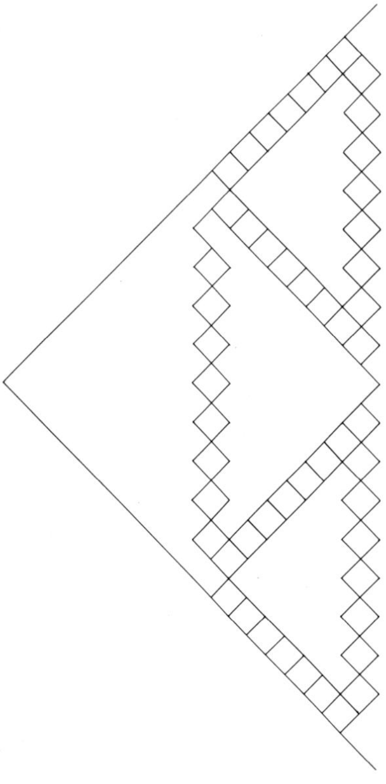

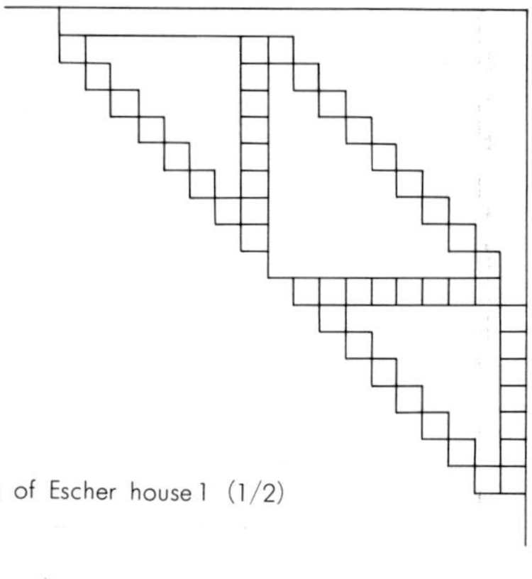

エッシャーの家1 断面図 Sections of Escher house 1 (1/2)

6 エッシャーの家1 Escher House 1 (1/2)

7 エッシャーの家2 Escher House 2 (1/2)

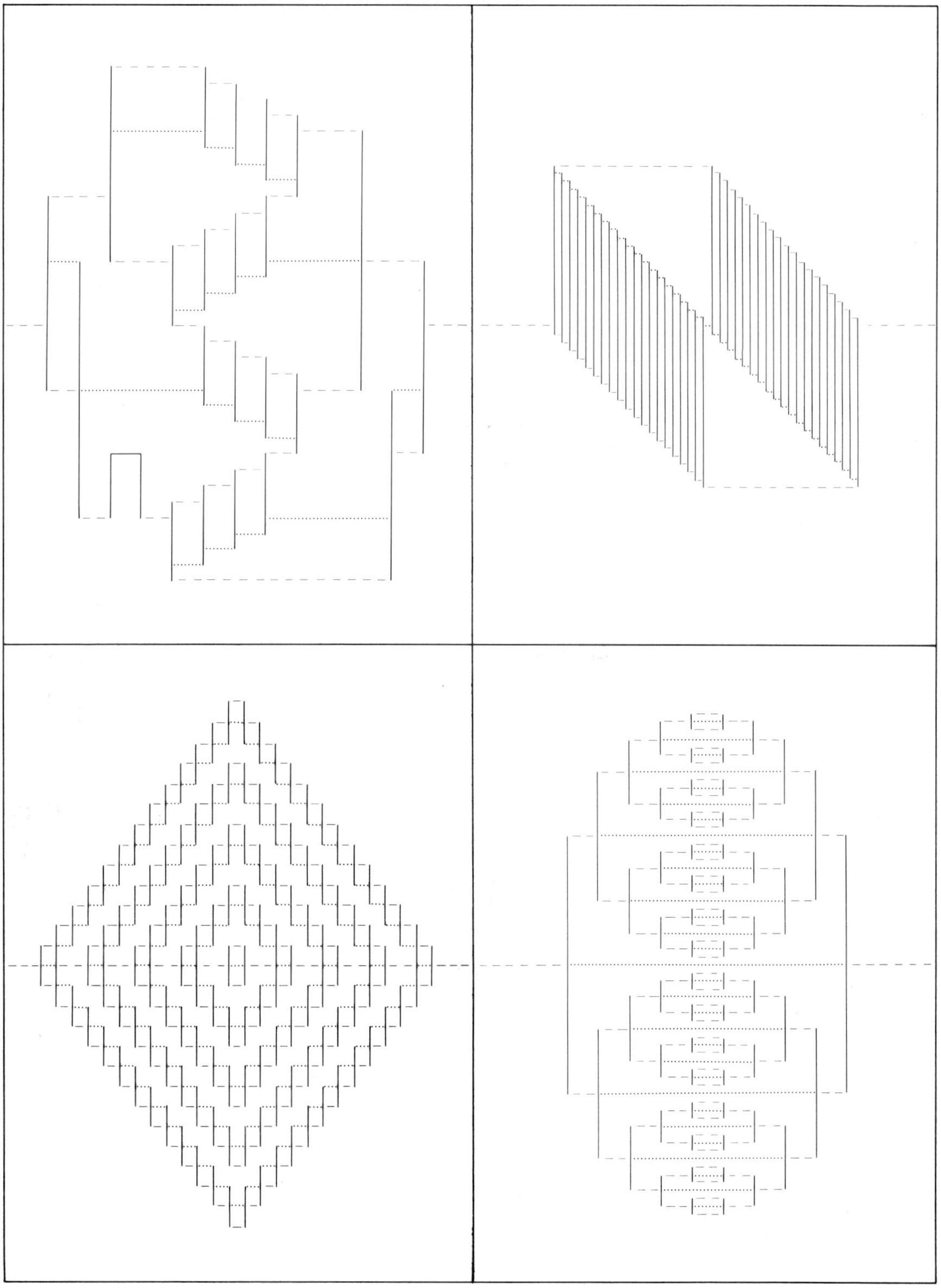

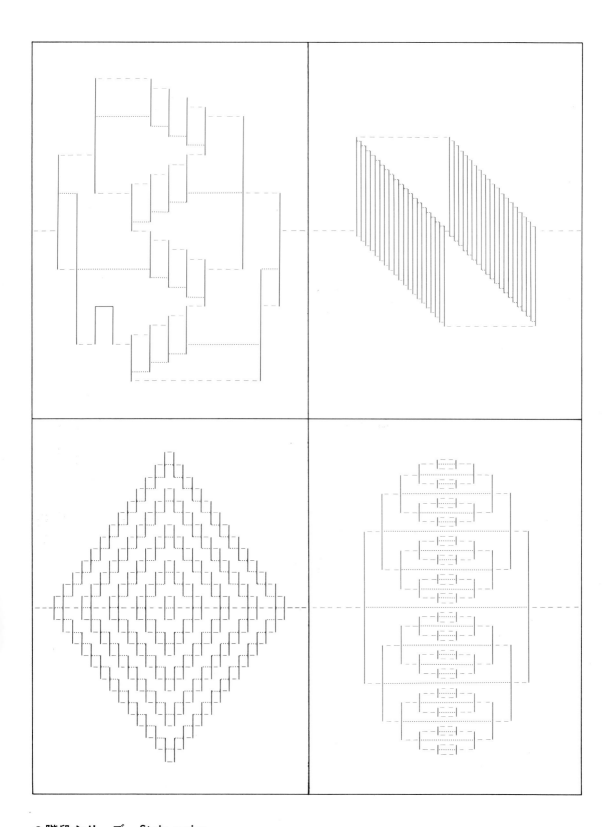

●階段シリーズ　Stair series

8　**白い舞台**　White stage (1/2)

9　**ブロック**　Block (1/2)

10　**蜂の巣**　Honeycomb (1/2)

11　**マヤの階段**　Mayan pyramid (1/2)

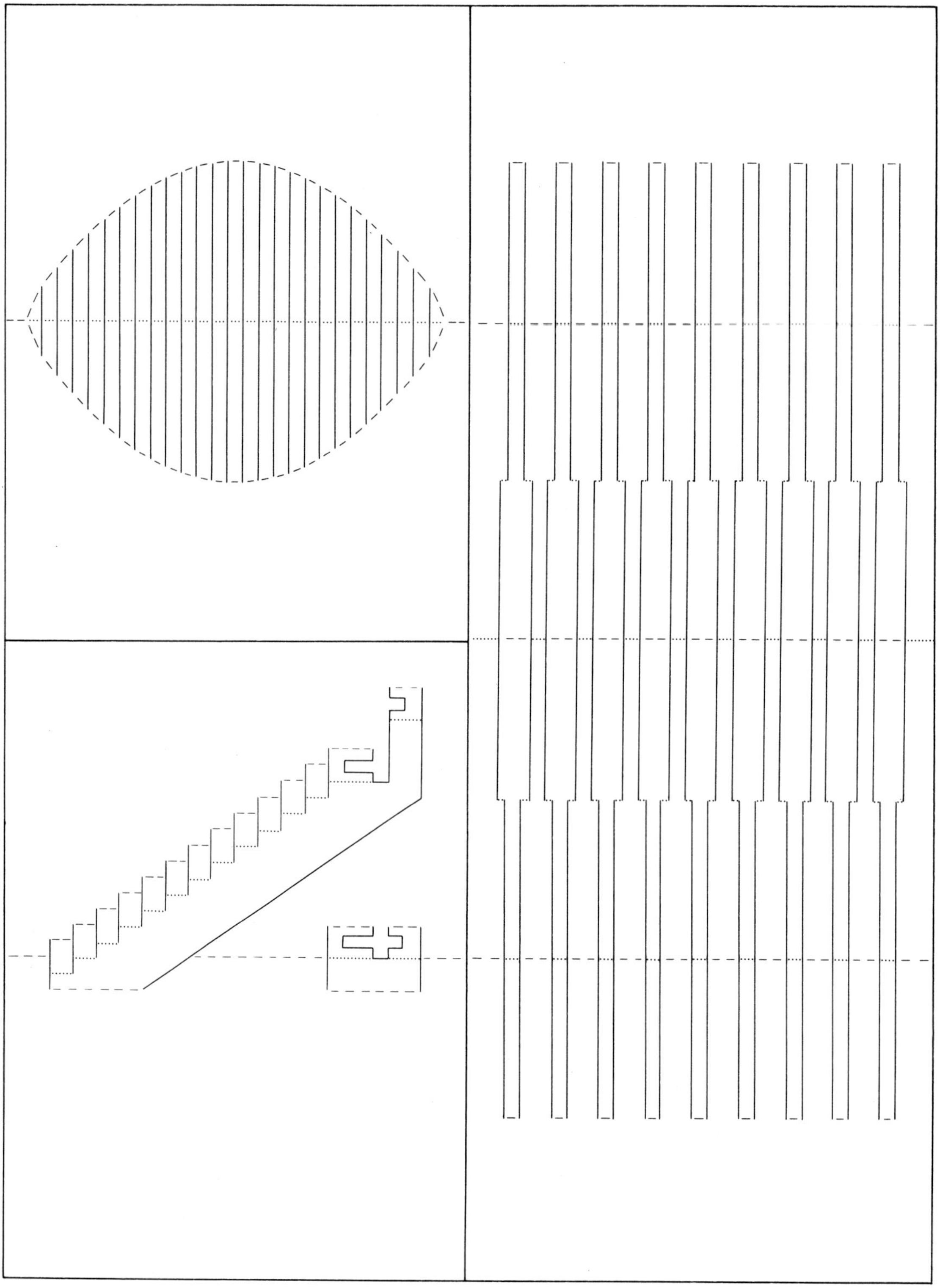

12 貝の音階 Shell music (1/2)
13 十三階段 Stairway to hell (1/2)

●パターン シリーズ Pattern series
14 すだれ Screen (1/2)

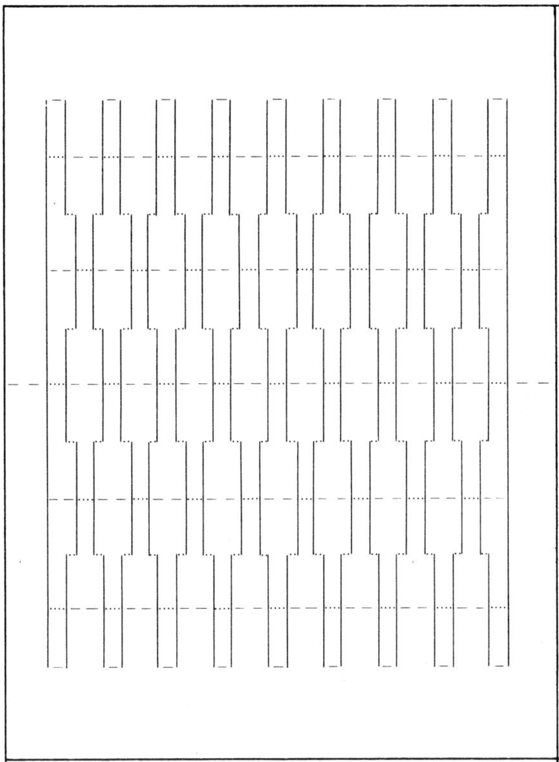

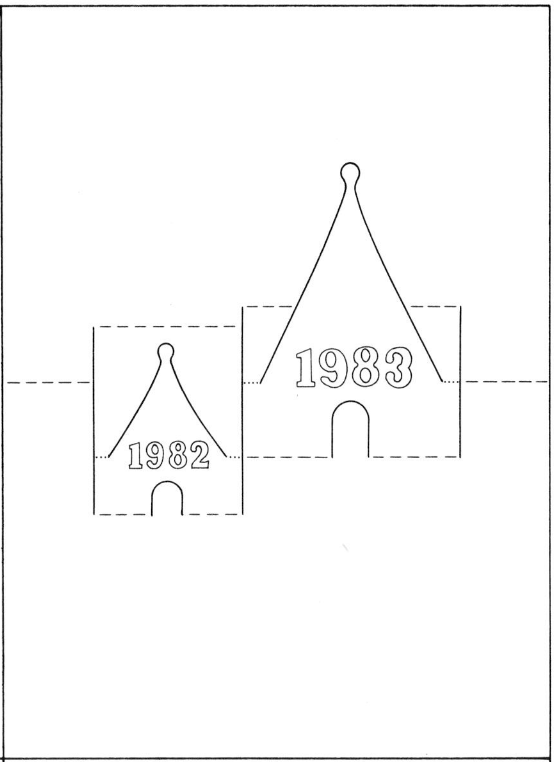

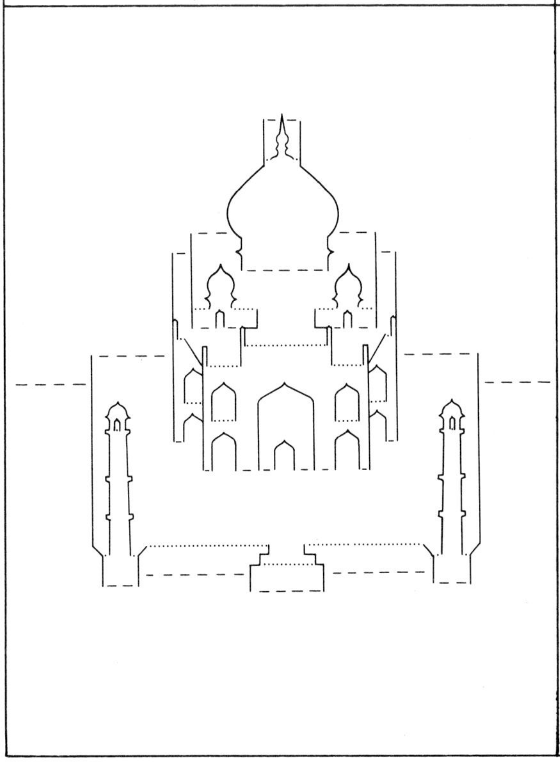

15 矢がすり Slit and arrow (1/2)
17 タージマハール Taj Mahal (1/2)

●建築シリーズ1 Architecture series 1

16 アフリカの家 African hut (1/2)
18 ロンドンの下町 London rowhouses (1/2)

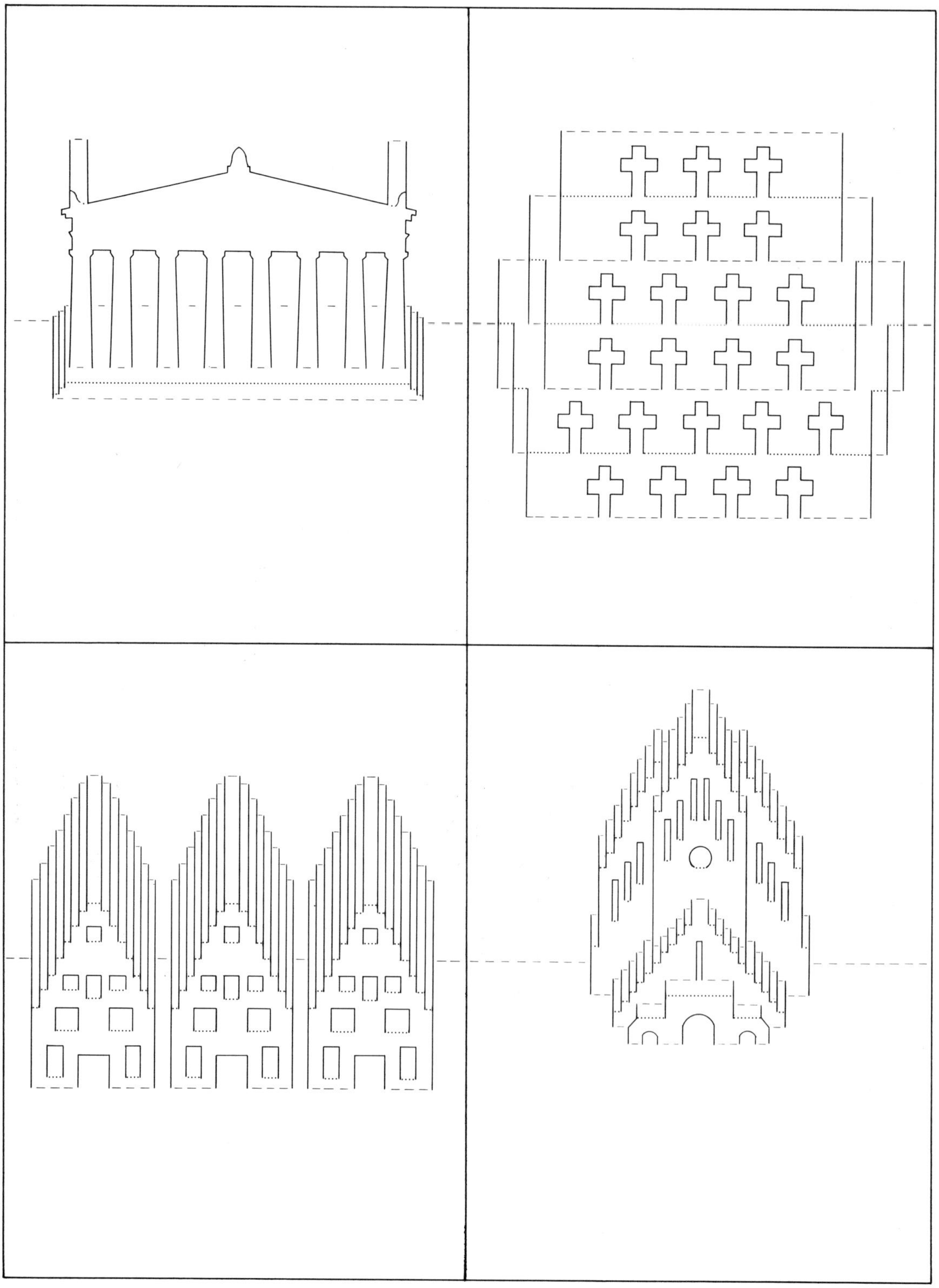

19 パルテノン Parthenon (1/2)
20 十字ヶ丘の分譲地 Necropolis (1/2)
22 アムステルダム Amsterdam façade (1/2)
23 オルガン教会 Organ church (1/2)

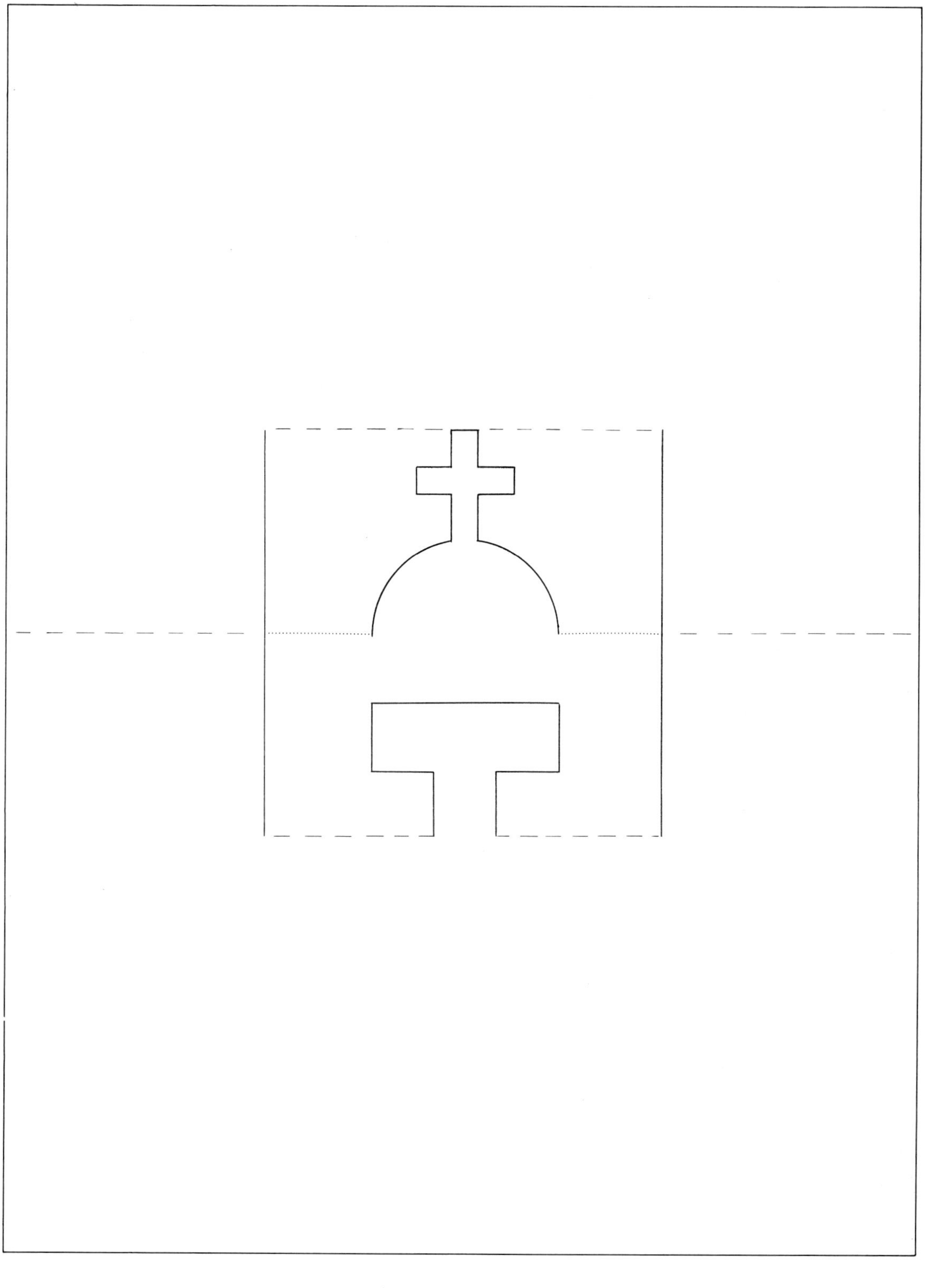

21　ミコノス　Mikonos (1/1)

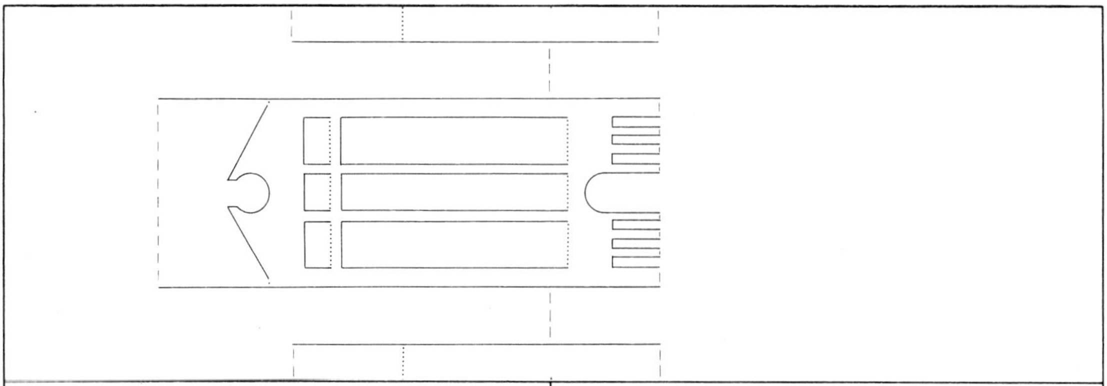

ウェディングパレスの量産用型板。コンピュータ
ー・レーザーで焼いた溝に刃を植えてあります。
Cutting plate of Wedding palace

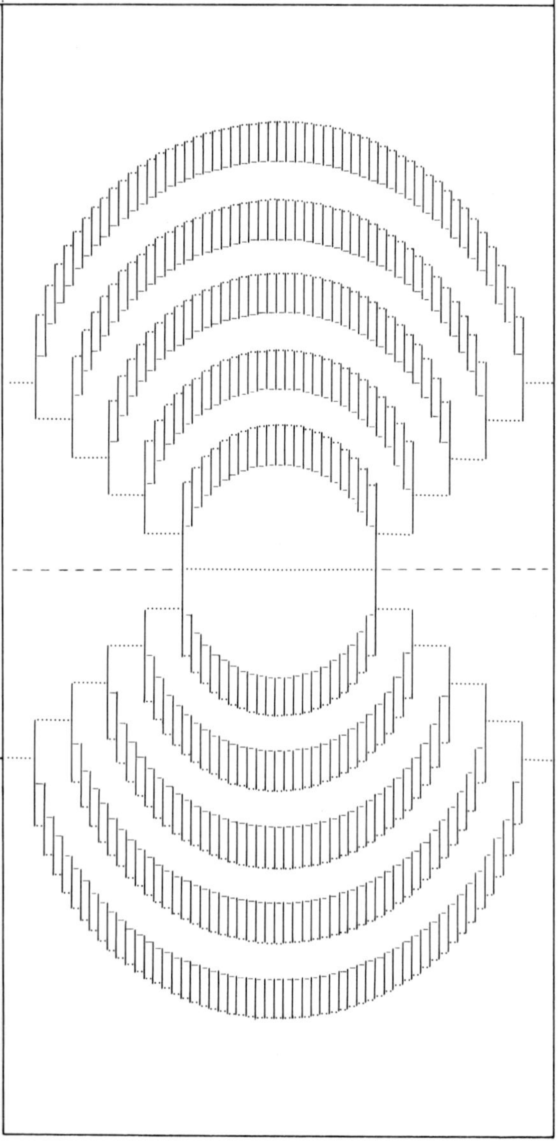

24 **ポストモダン** Post modern (1/2)
25 **ガラスのピラミッド** Glass pyramid (1/2)
27 **円型劇場** Amphitheatre (1/2)

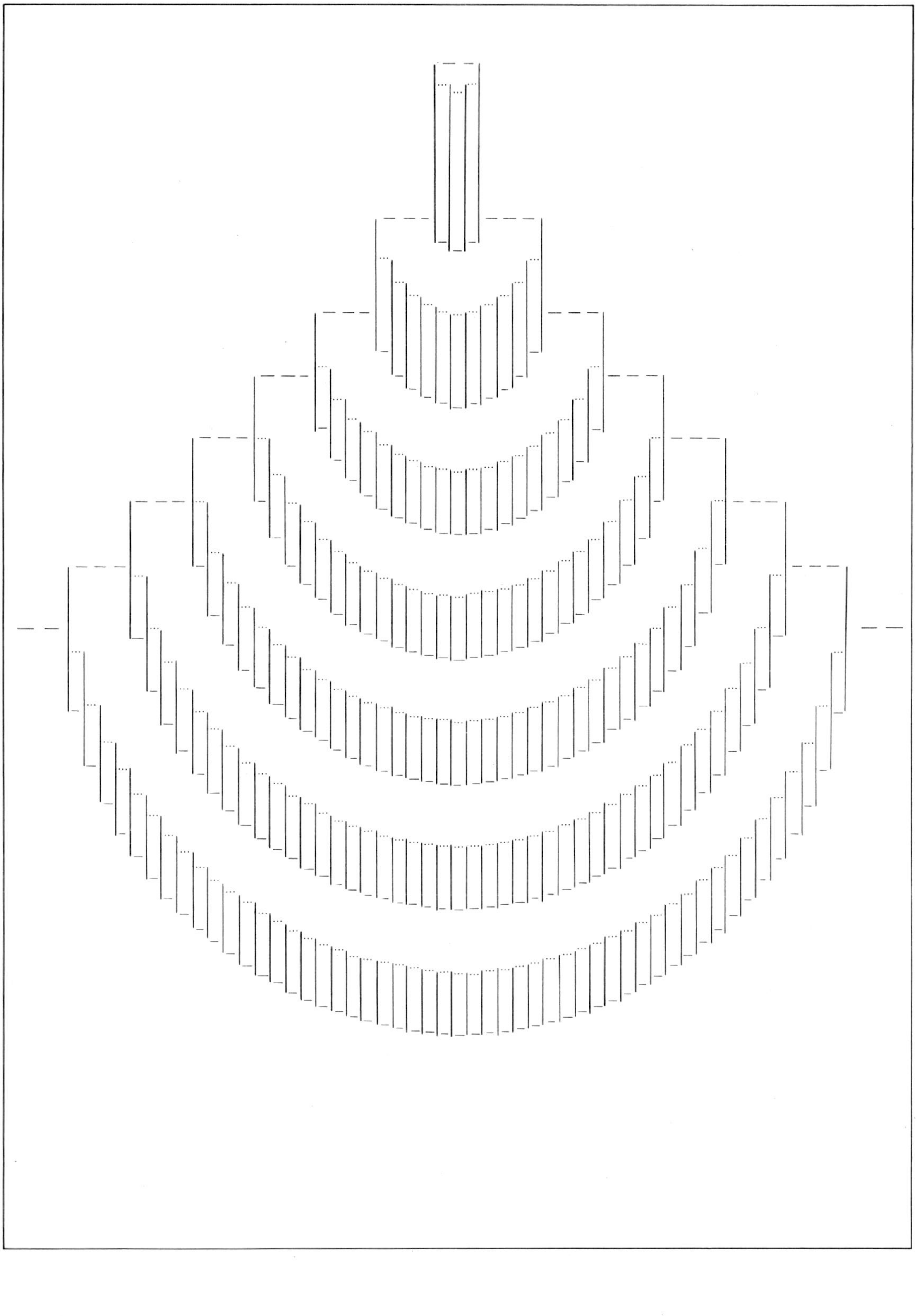

26 ウェディングパレス Wedding palace (1/1)

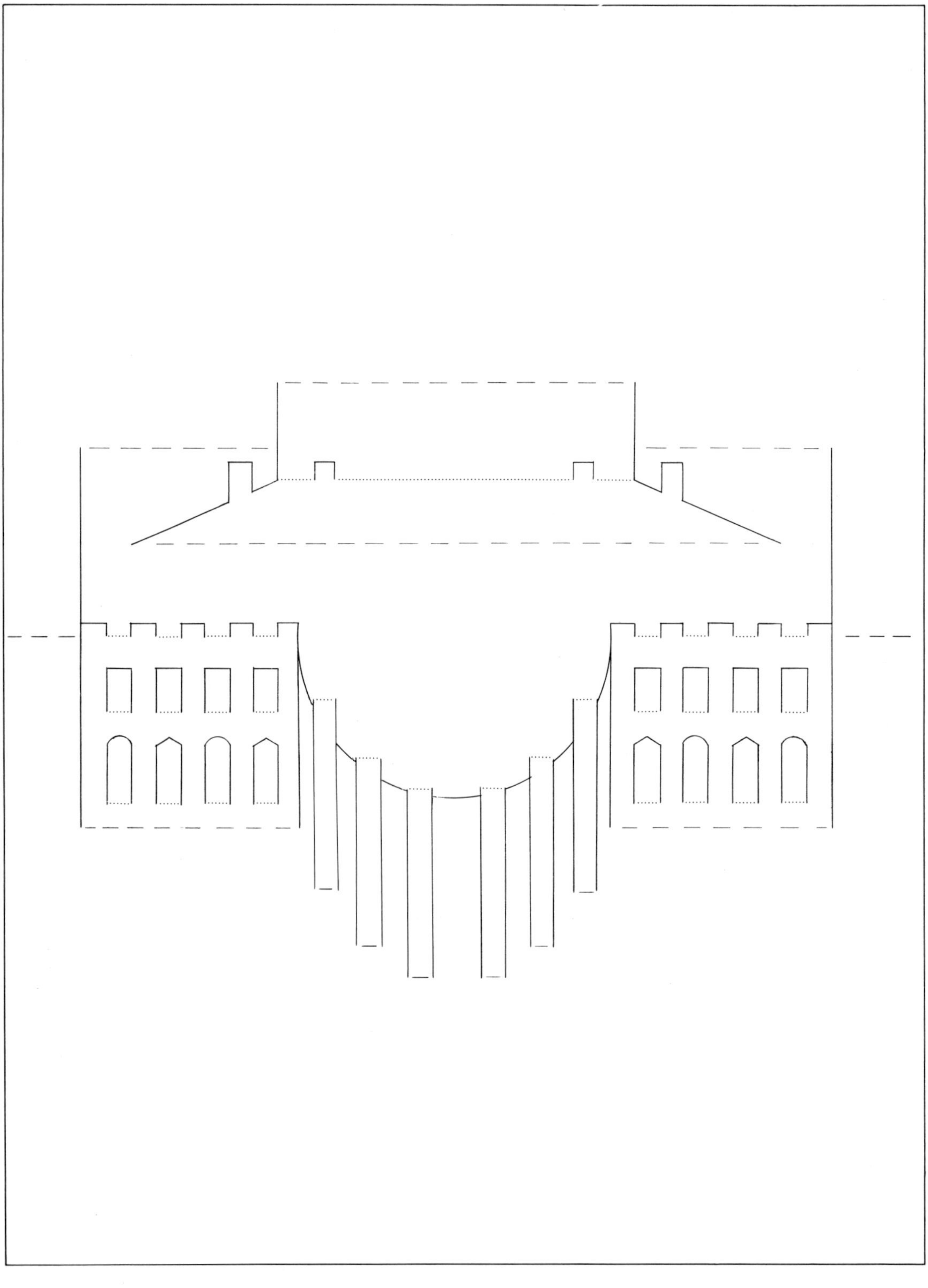

28　ホワイトハウス 1　The White House 1 (1/1)

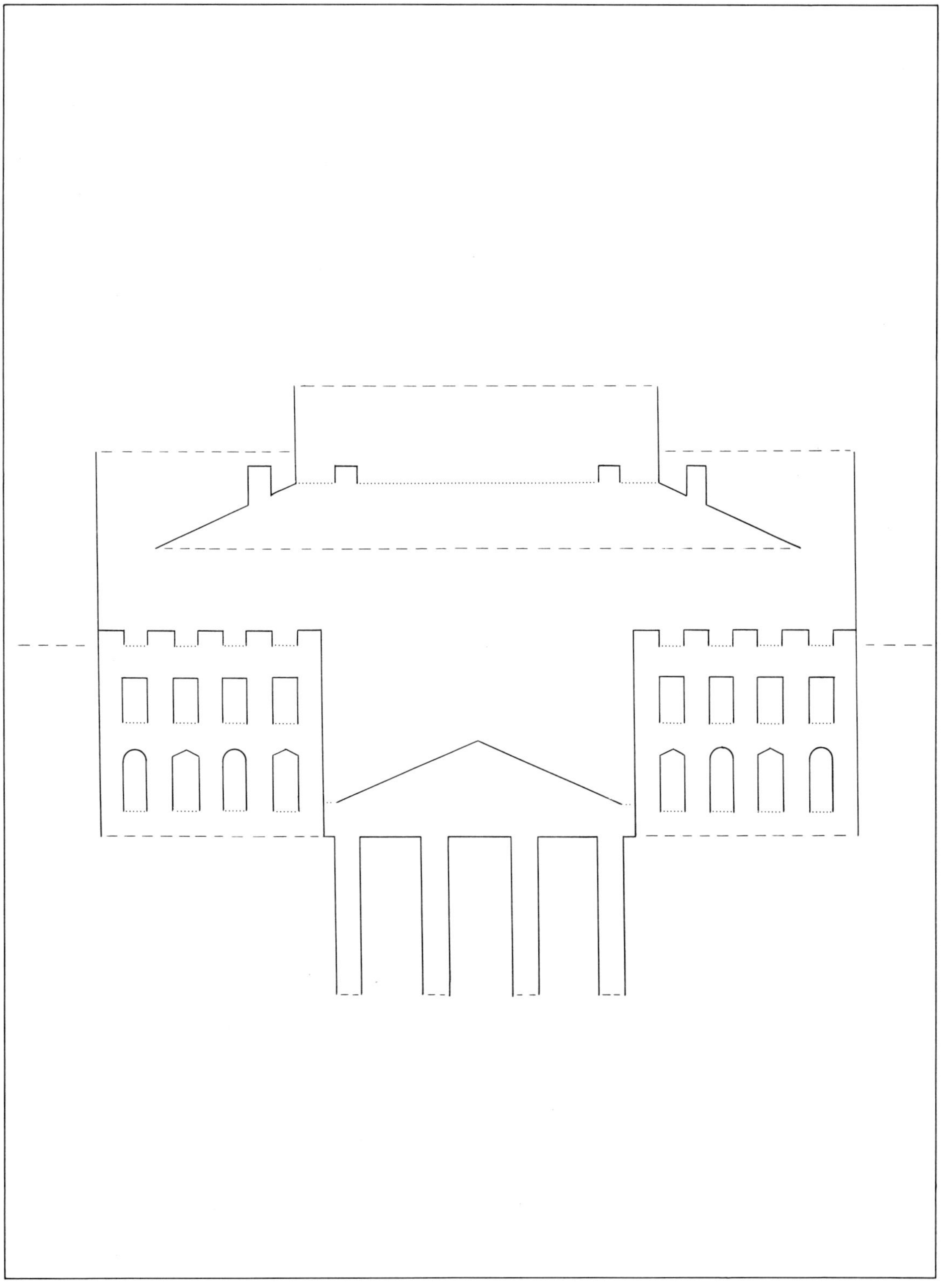

29　ホワイトハウス 2　The White House 2 (1/1)

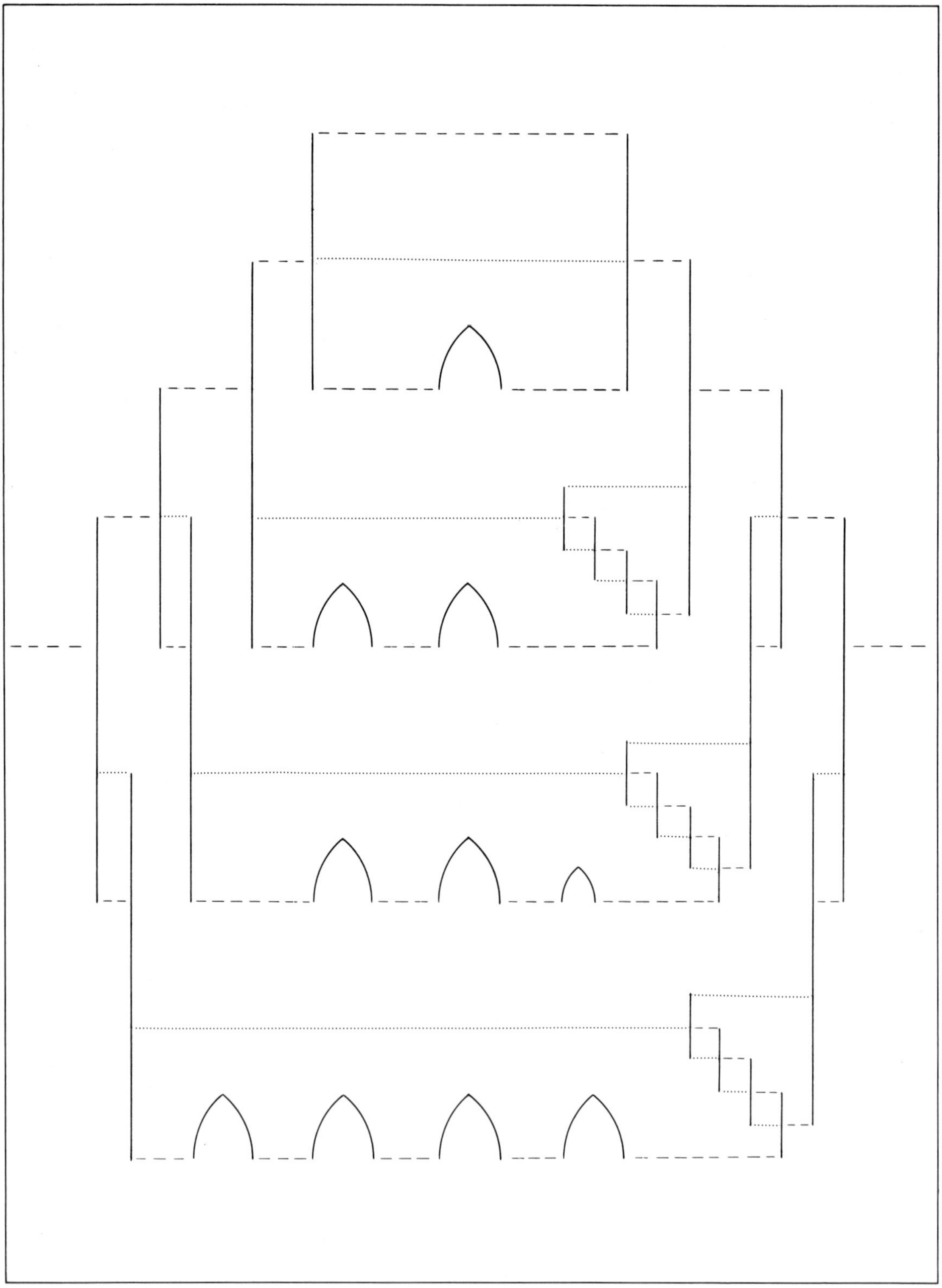

●穴の家シリーズ　Cave series
30· 崖の家　Cliff house (1/1)

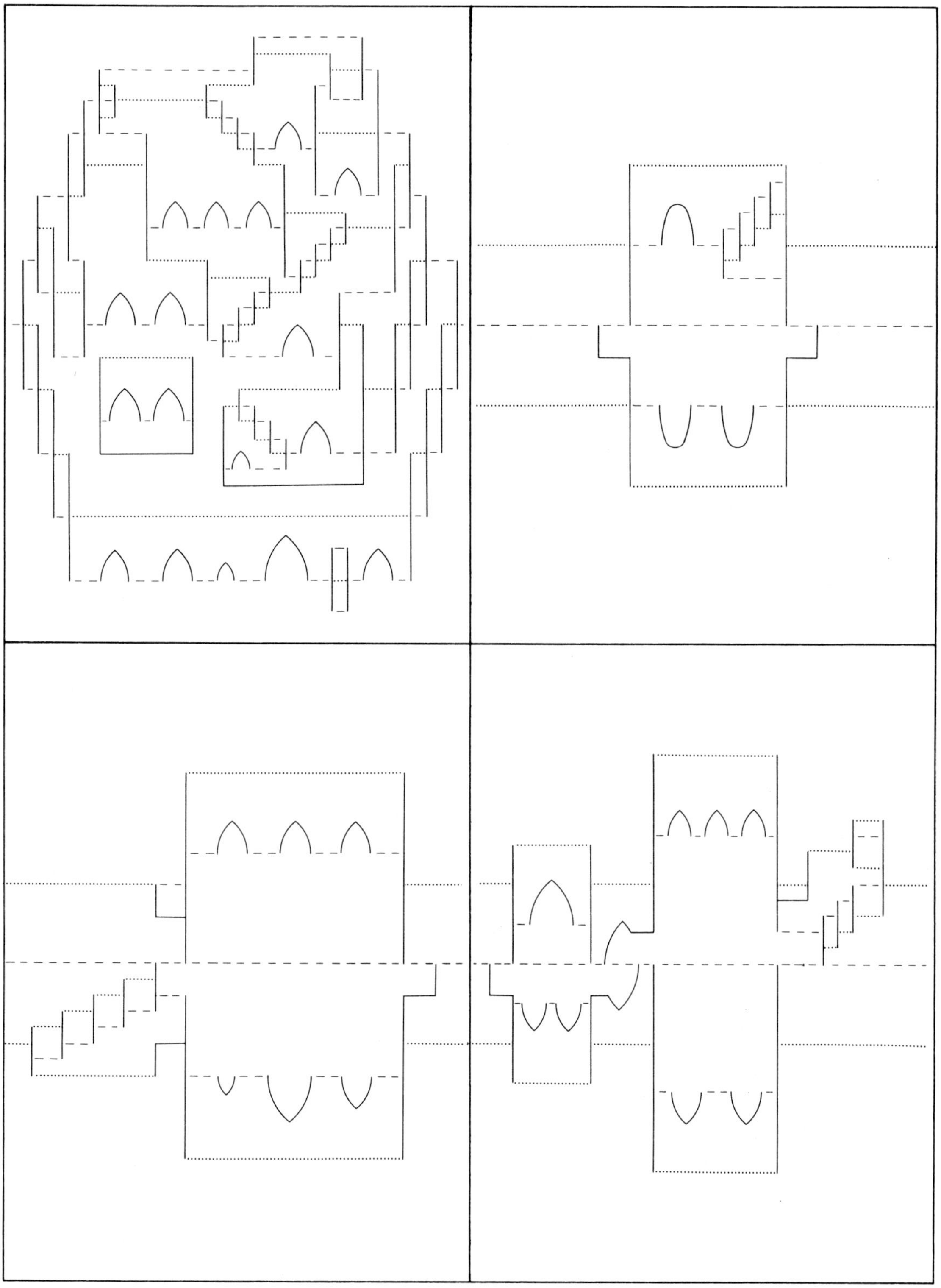

31 **龍宮城** Palace of seagoddess (1/2)

32 **地下の家1** Underground house 1 (1/2)

33 **地下の家2** Underground house 2 (1/2)

34 **地下の家3** Underground house 3 (1/2)

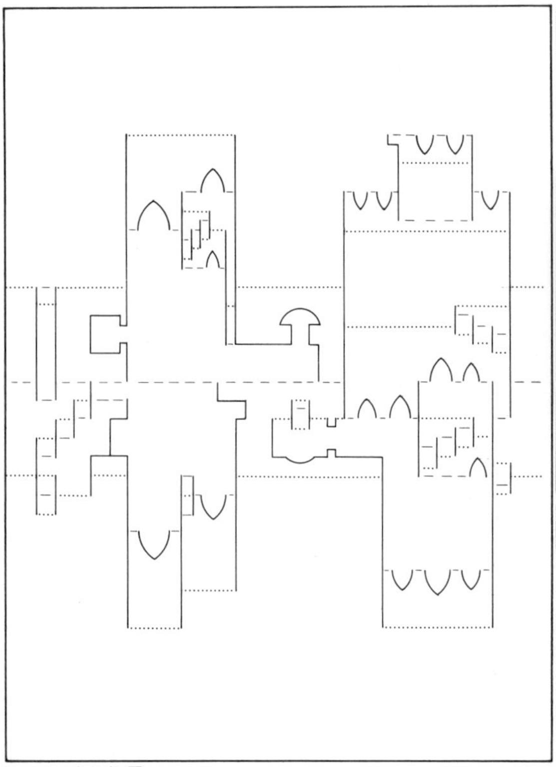

中国の地下住居

黄河中流の黄土地帯には，5千年の歴史をもつ珍しい地下窰洞集落があり，今なお4千万人が住んでいます。かねての願いがかなって1981～3年にデザイン・サーヴェイを行いました。窰洞住居には崖に掘った横穴に住む山懸式と，高原の平地にまず7m角ほどの竪穴を掘り，それを中庭として横穴で囲む下沈式とがあり，30～31は山懸式，32～35は下沈式，31は併用形式です。学校・病院・工場・倉庫など多目的に，冬暖かく夏涼しく過ごせる省エネルギーシェルターとして注目されます。下沈式は，折り紙で立体が飛び出す仕組みを裏返した，ネガティブな造形になっています。

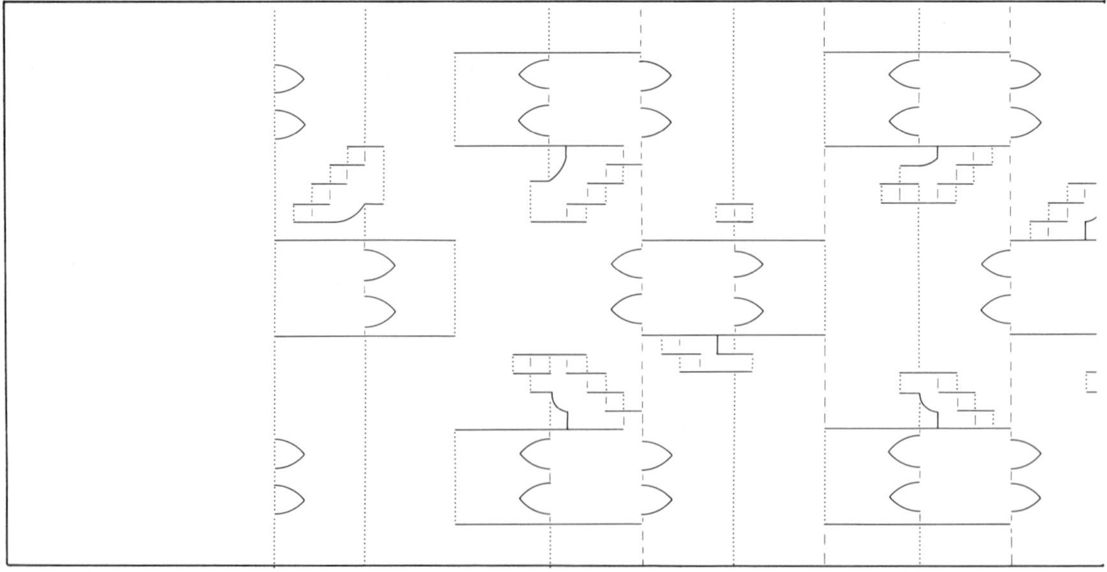

35　**地下の家4**　Underground house 4 (1/2)
37　**地下の村2**　Underground village 2 (1/2)

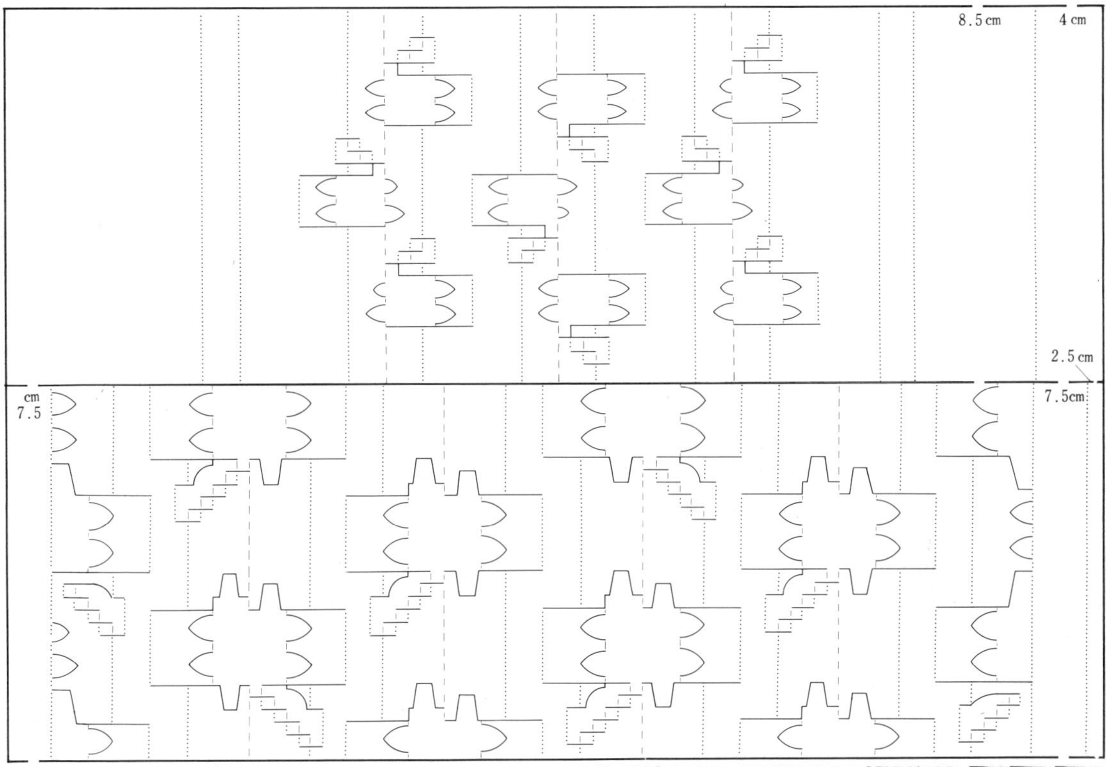

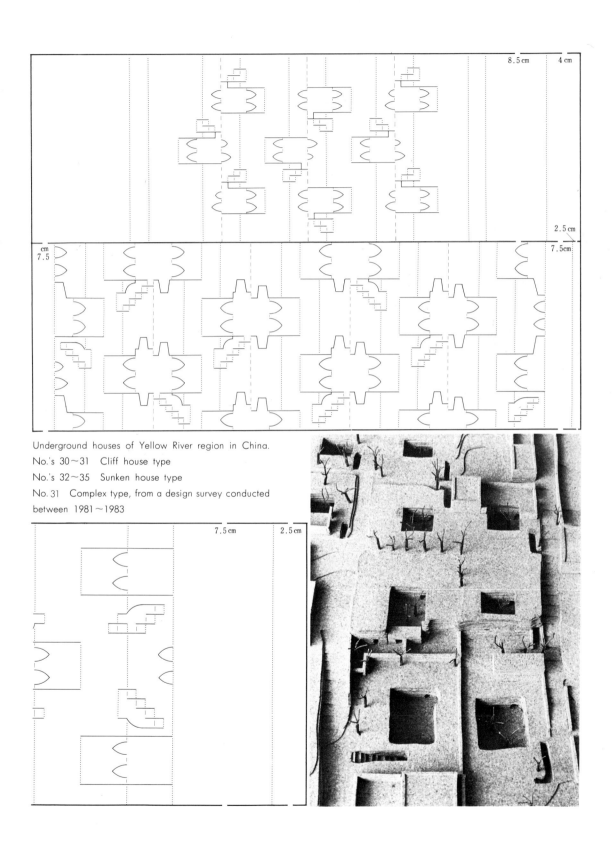

Underground houses of Yellow River region in China.
No.'s 30～31 Cliff house type
No.'s 32～35 Sunken house type
No. 31 Complex type, from a design survey conducted between 1981～1983

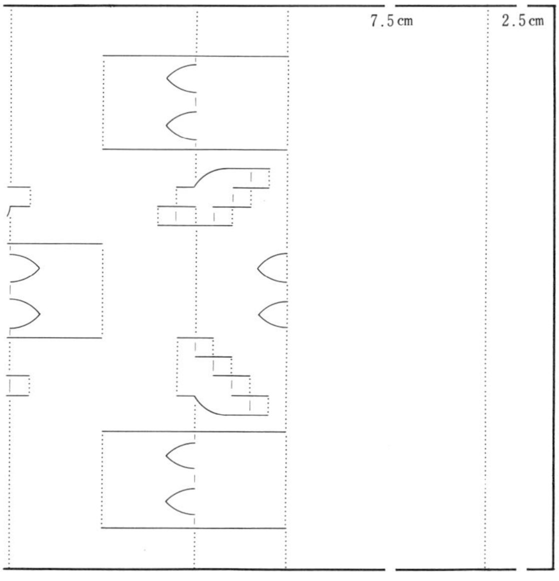

36 **地下の村 1** Underground village 1 (1/3)
38 **地下の村 3** Underground village 3 (1/3)

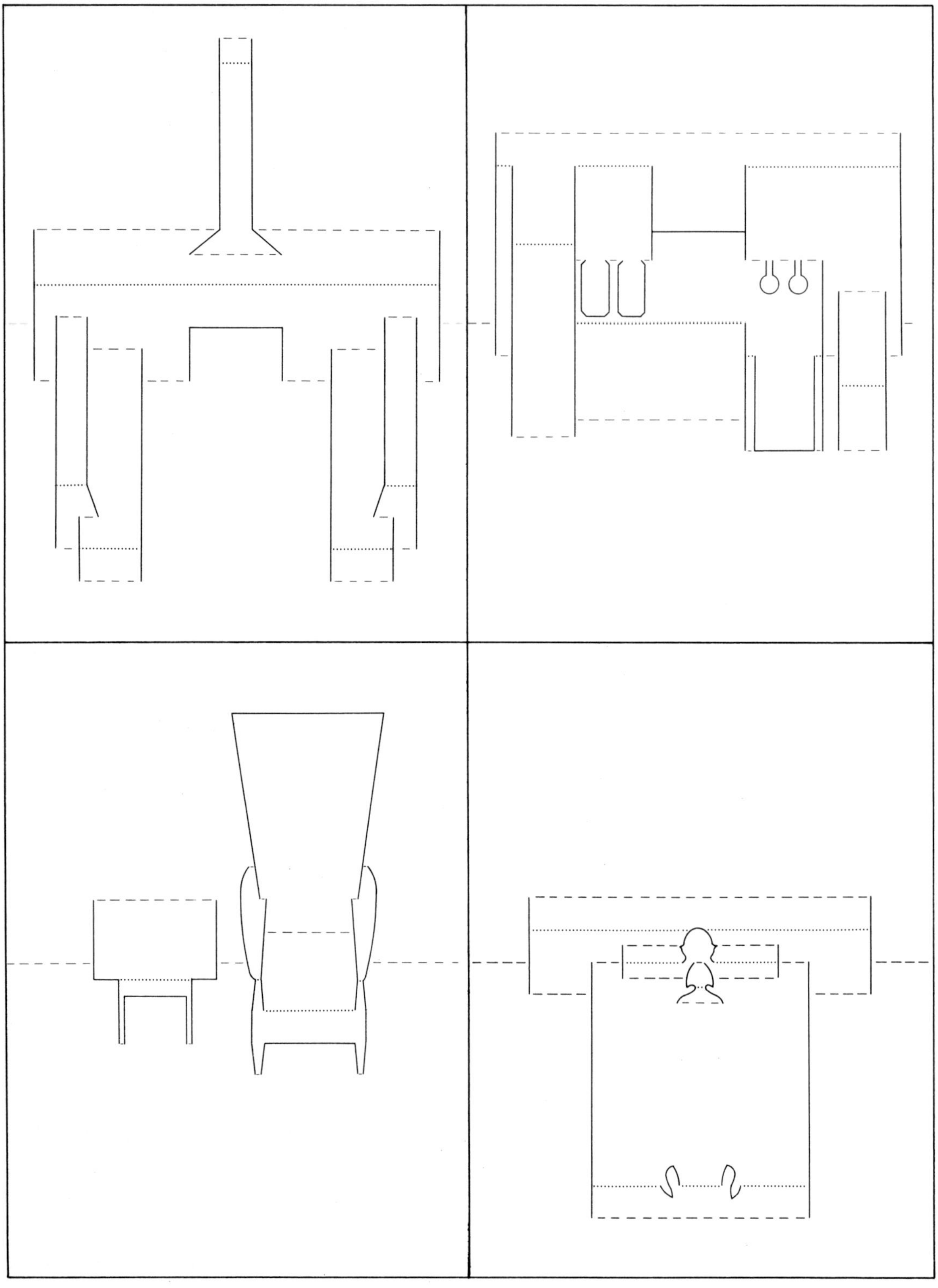

●インテリア シリーズ　Interior series

39　炉辺談話　Living room (1/2)

40　キッチン　Kitchen (1/2)

41　インテリア　Interior (1/2)

42　ベッドルーム　Bed room (1/2)

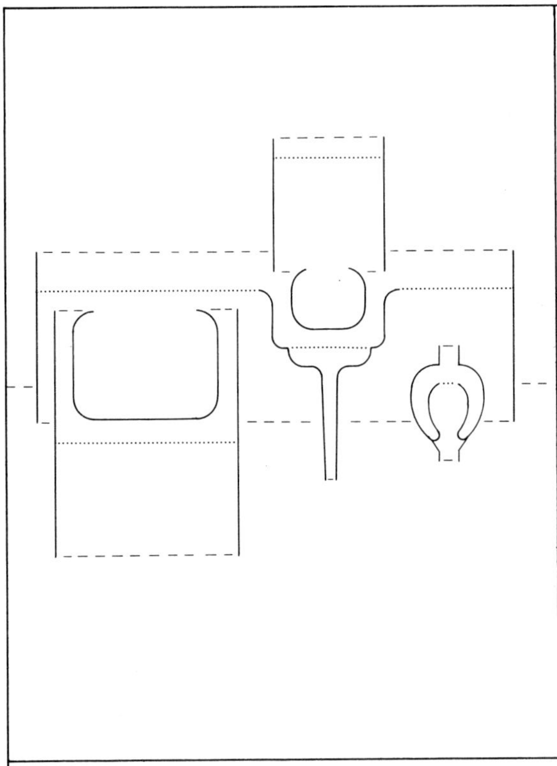

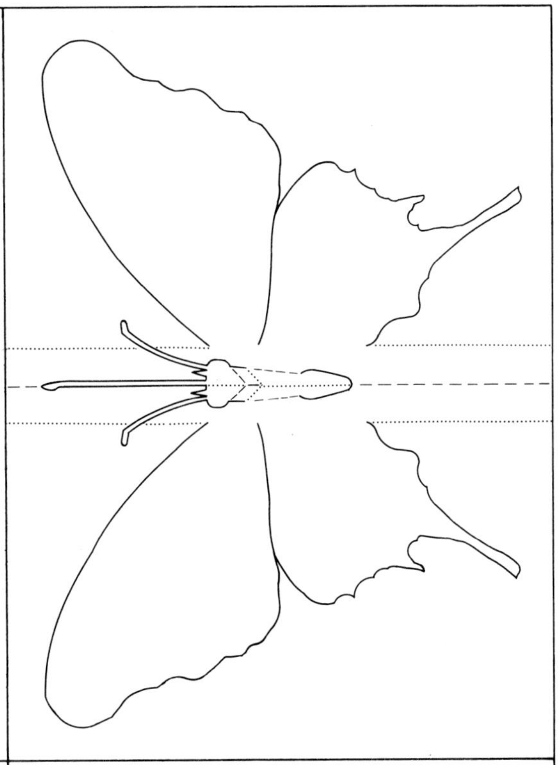

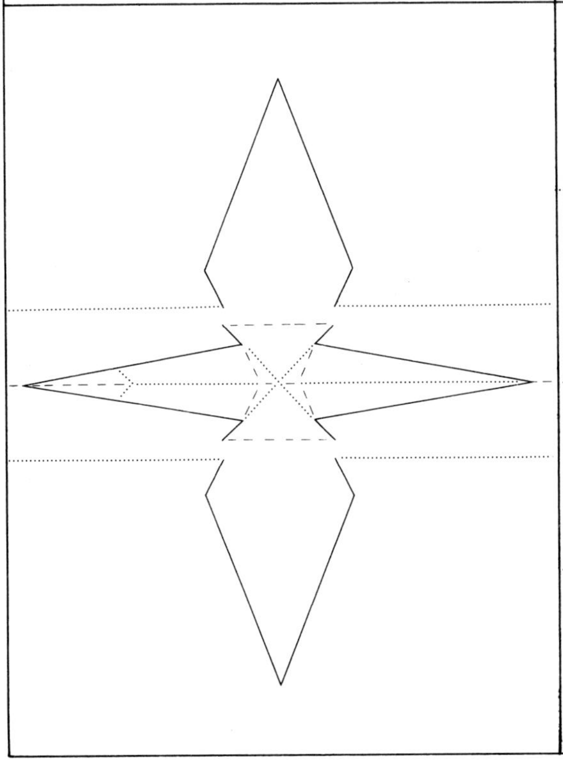

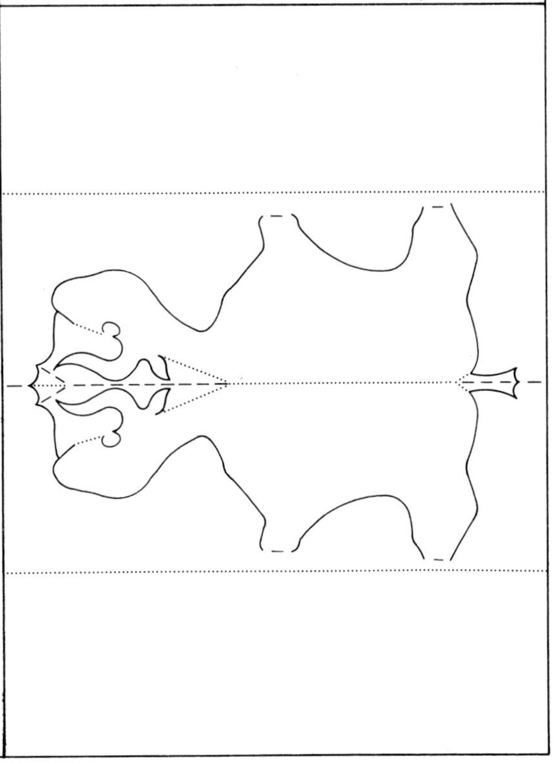

●生物シリーズ　Biomorphose series

43　バスルーム　Bath room (1/2)

44　蝶　Papillon (1/2)

45　鶴　Crane (1/2)

46　丑（牛）　Cattle (1/2)

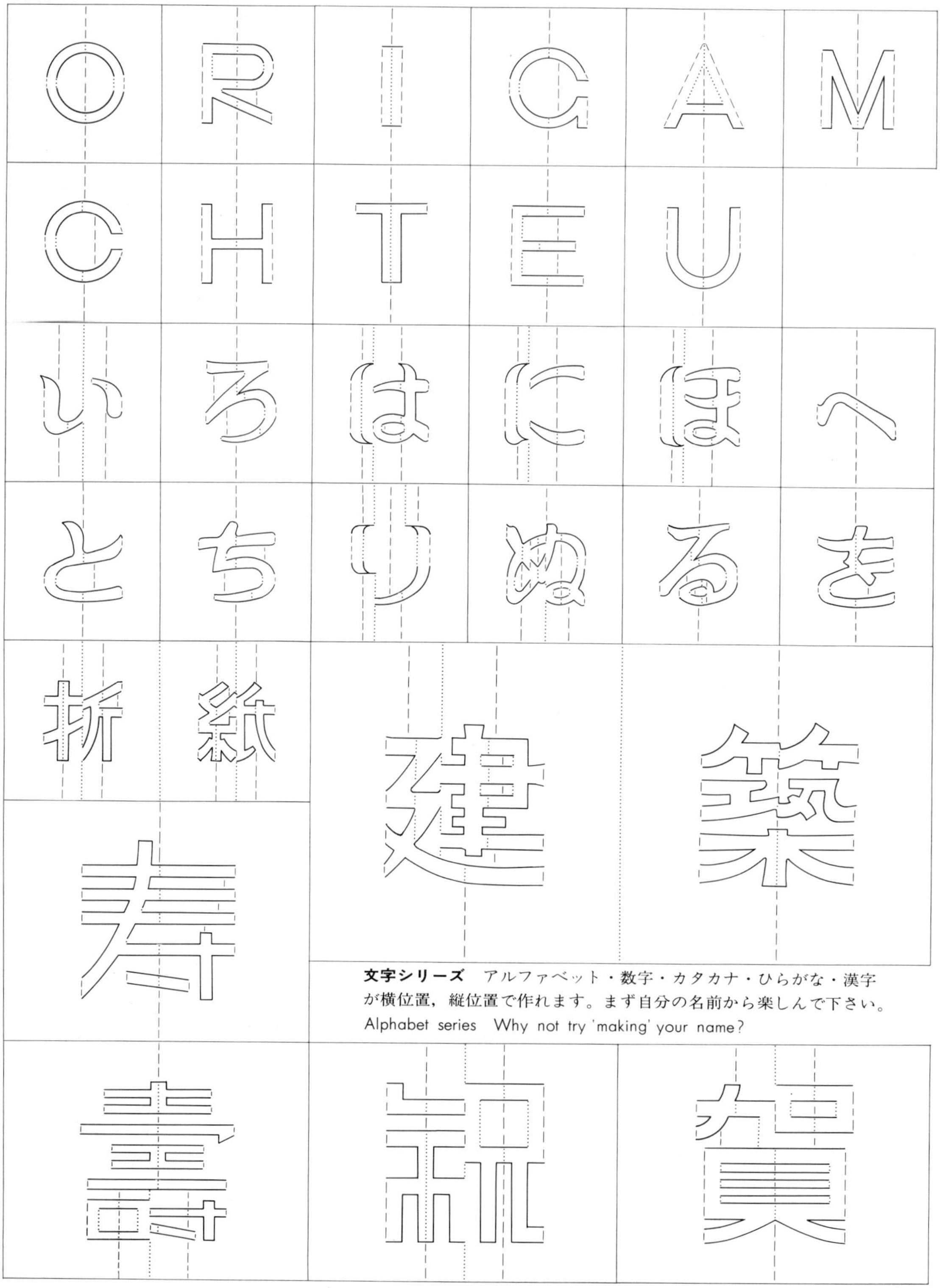

文字シリーズ　アルファベット・数字・カタカナ・ひらがな・漢字が横位置，縦位置で作れます。まず自分の名前から楽しんで下さい。
Alphabet series　Why not try 'making' your name?

●文字シリーズ　Alphabet series

47　ORIGAMCHTEU (1/4)
48　**いろはにほへとちりぬるを**　Japanese alphabet (1/4)
49　**折紙建築**　Origamic Architecture (1/4) (1/2)
50　**寿**　Good luck 1 (1/4)
51　**壽**　Good luck 2 (1/4)
52　**祝**　Celebration (1/4)
53　**賀**　Congratulation (1/4)

● **立体シリーズ　Void solid series**

54　シドニーオペラハウス　Sydney opera house（1/1）

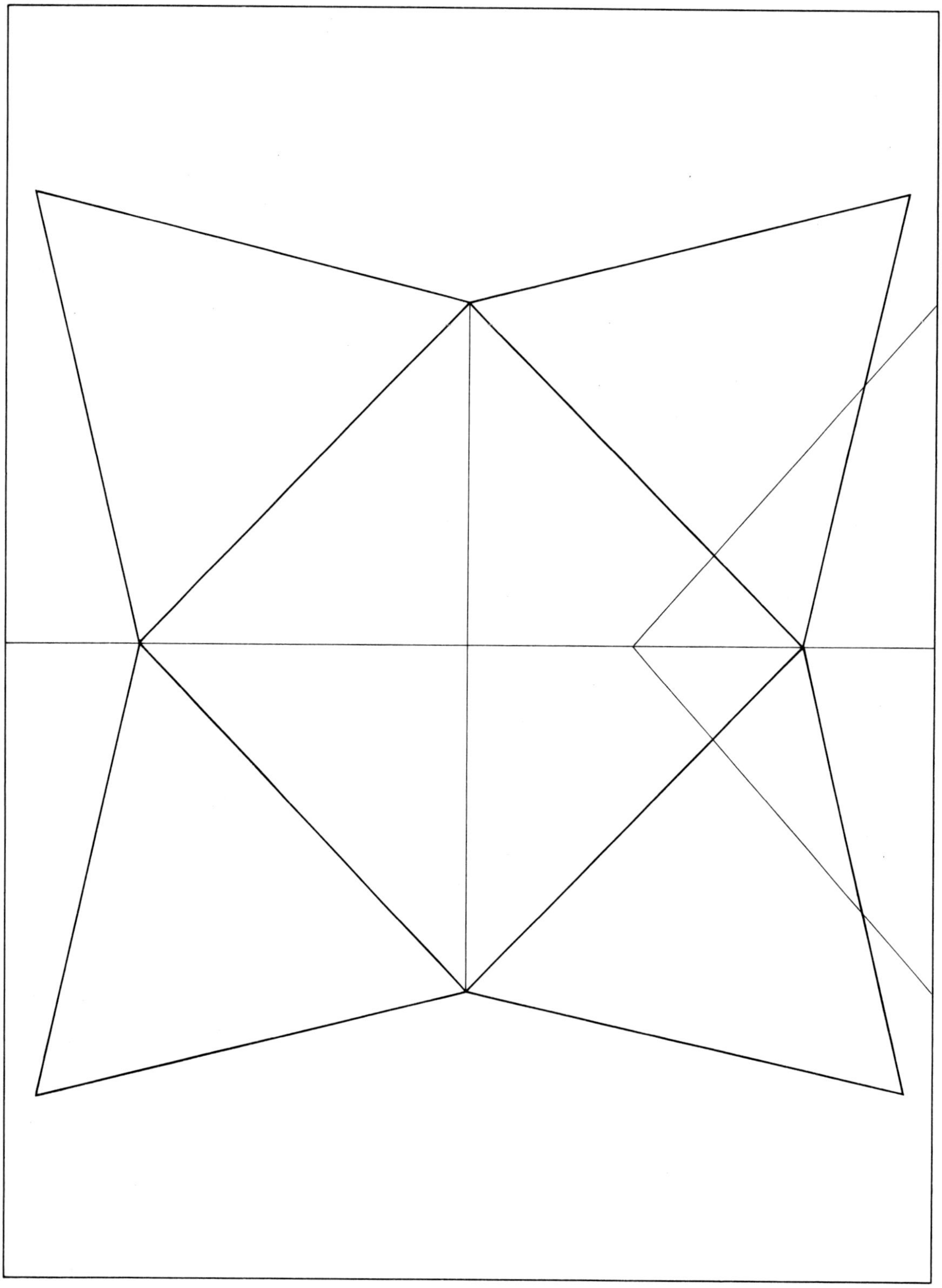

56 ピラミッド 2 Pyramid 2 (1/1)

55 ピラミッド1 Pyramid 1 (1/2)
57 精霊の家 Spirit house (1/2)
58 半球儀 1 Hemisphere 1 (1/2)
59 半球儀 2 Hemisphere 2 (1/2)

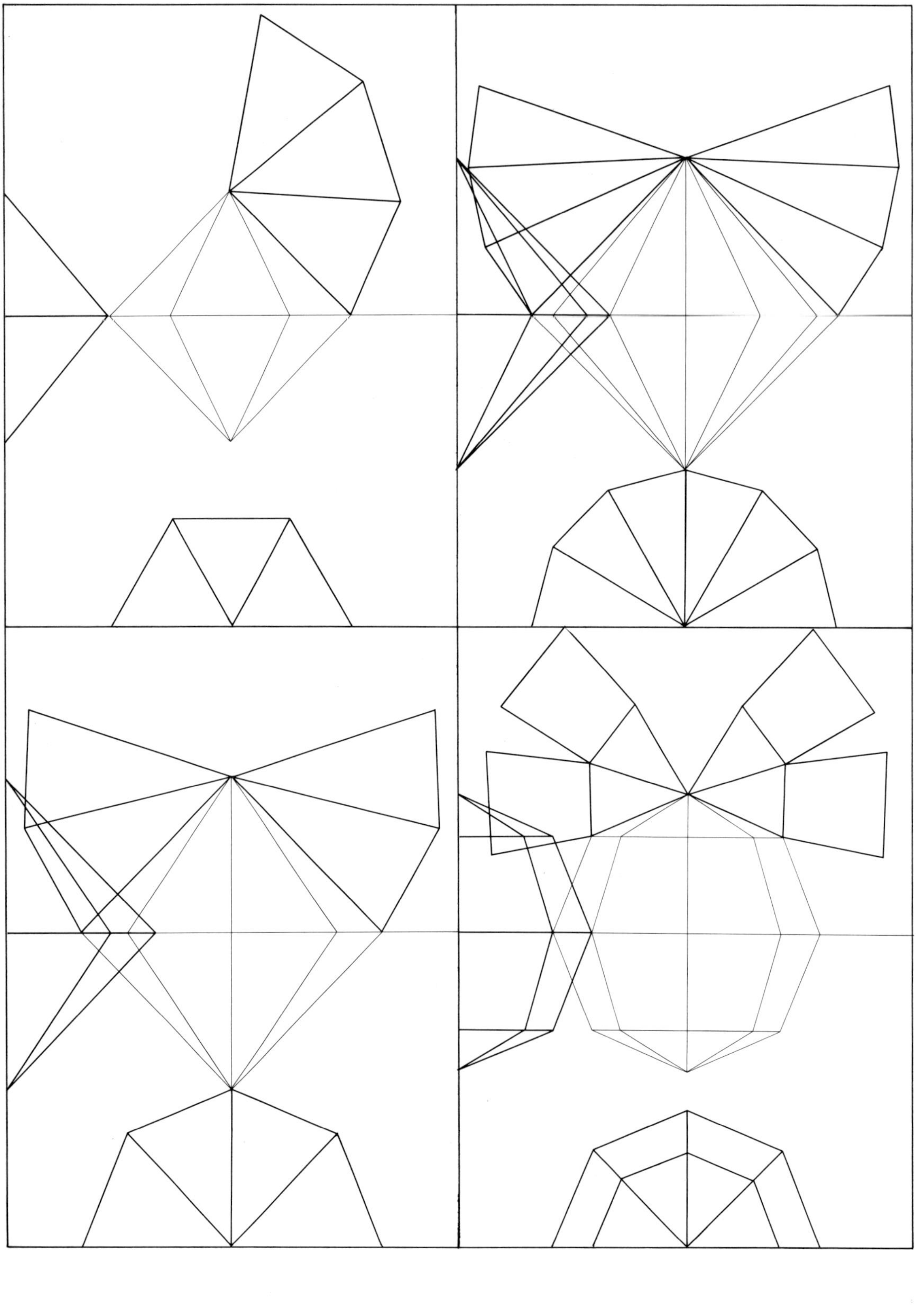

60 **半球儀3** Hemisphere 3 (1/2)

61 **半球儀4** Hemisphere 4 (1/2)

62 **半球儀5** Hemisphere 5 (1/2)

63 **半球儀6** Hemisphere 6 (1/2)

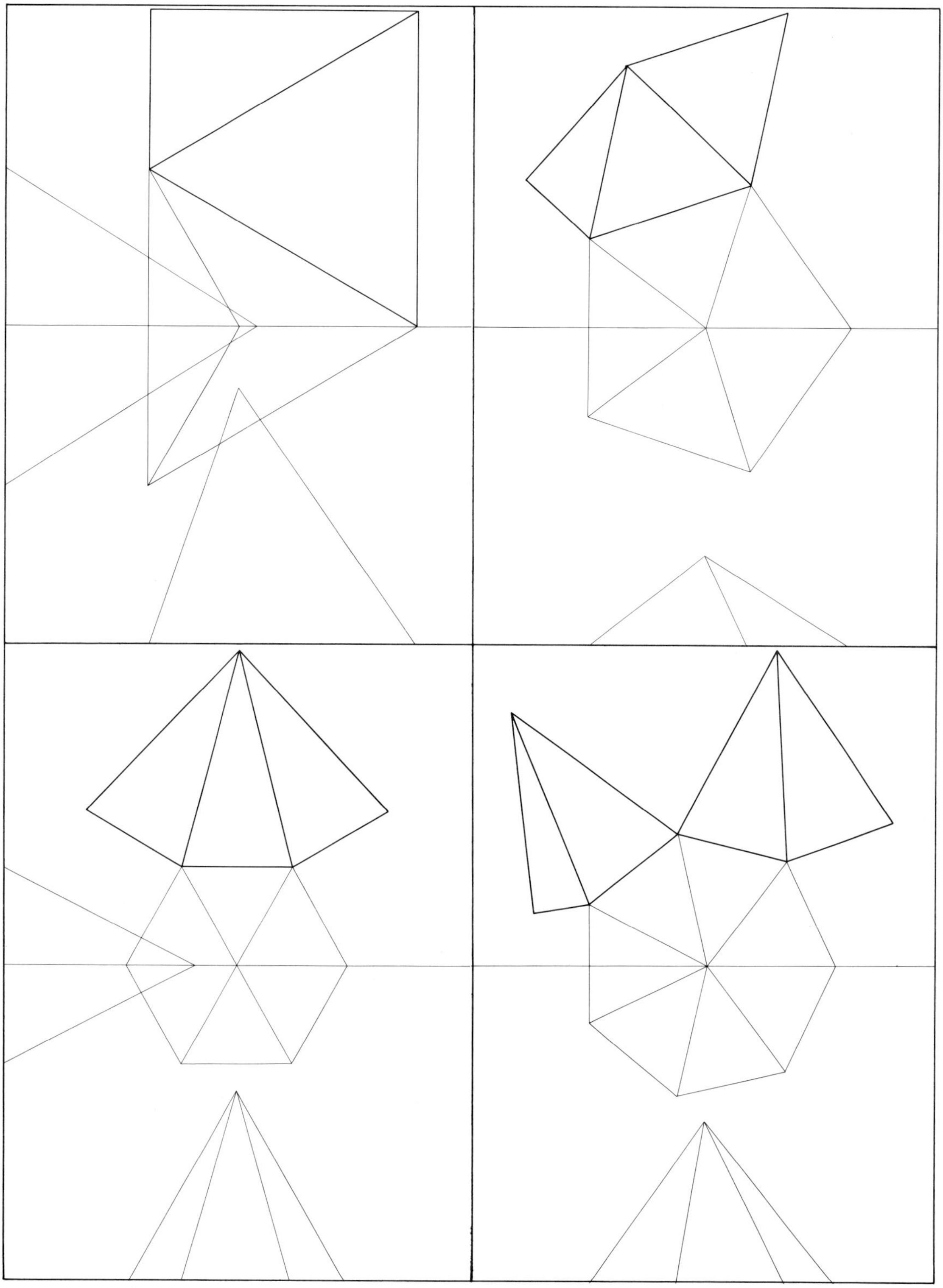

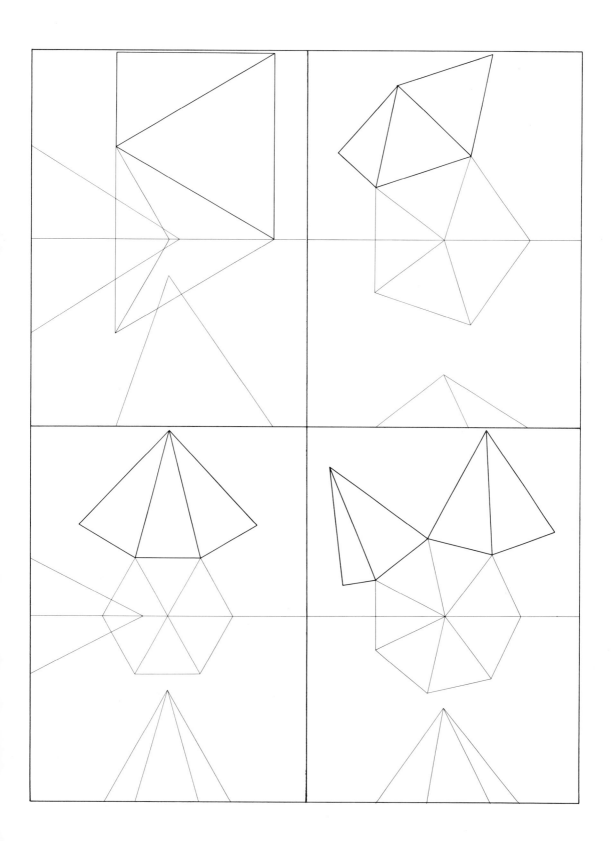

64 **三角錐** Tetrahedron (1/2)
65 **五角錐** Pentagonal pyramid (1/2)
66 **六角錐** Hexagonal pyramid (1/2)
67 **七角錐** Heptagonal pyramid (1/2)

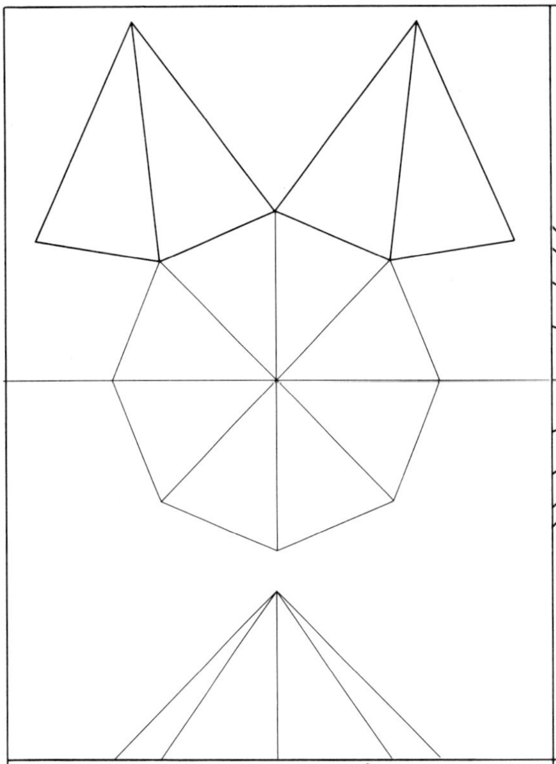

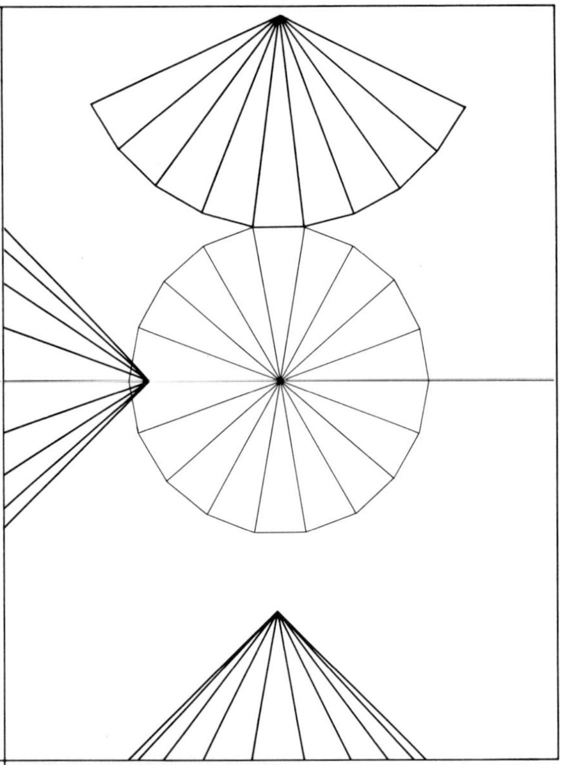

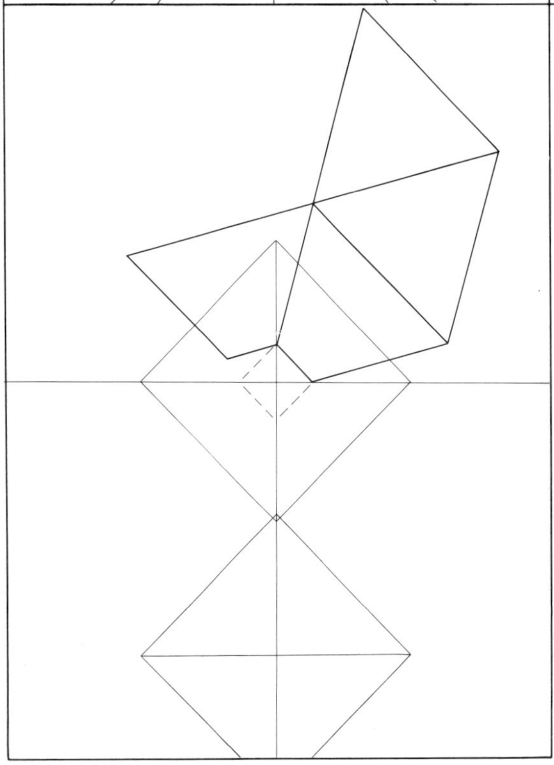

ピサの斜塔　1963年は支えに，1983年は押しに行って来ました。
Campanile of Pisa being supported in 1963 and being pushed in 1983.

68　八角錐　Octagonal pyramid (1/2)　　69　円錐　Cone (1/2)
70　地球儀　Globe (1/2)

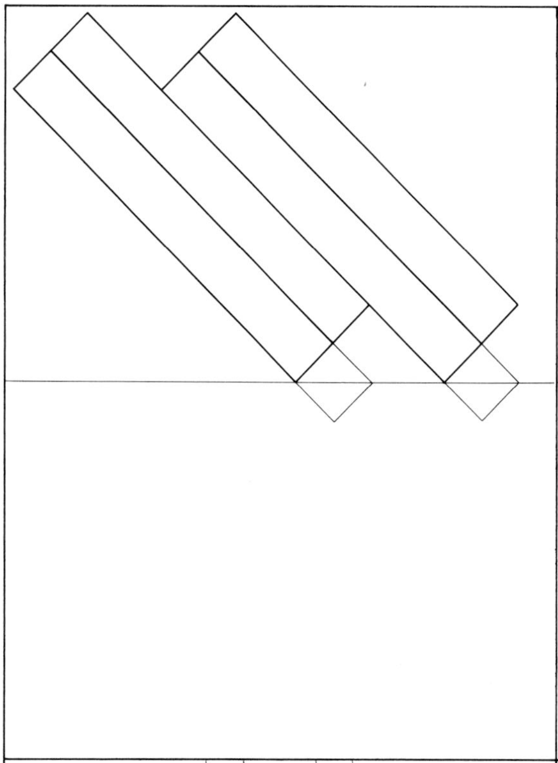

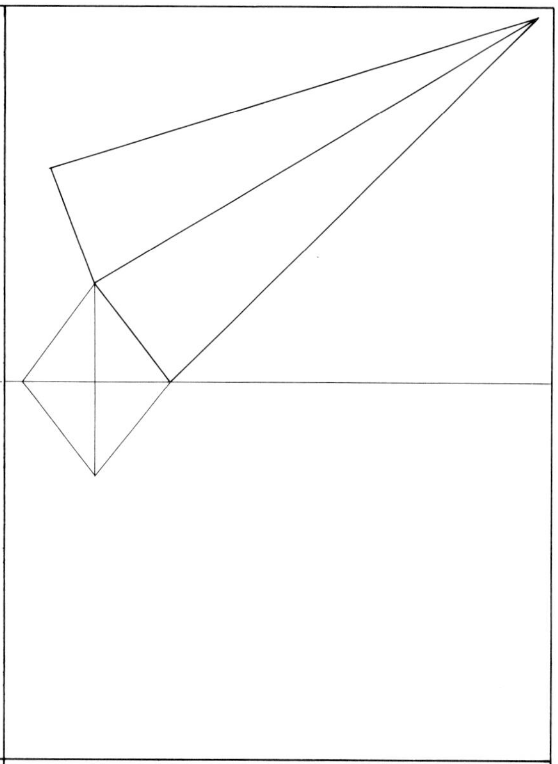

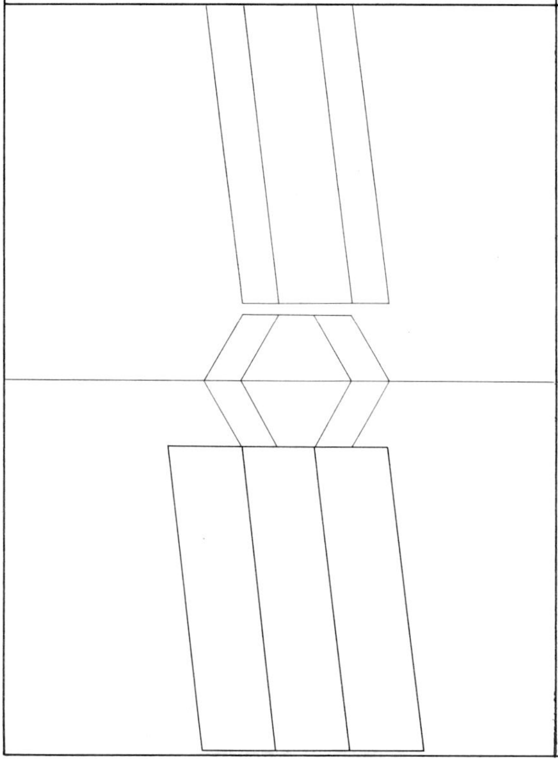

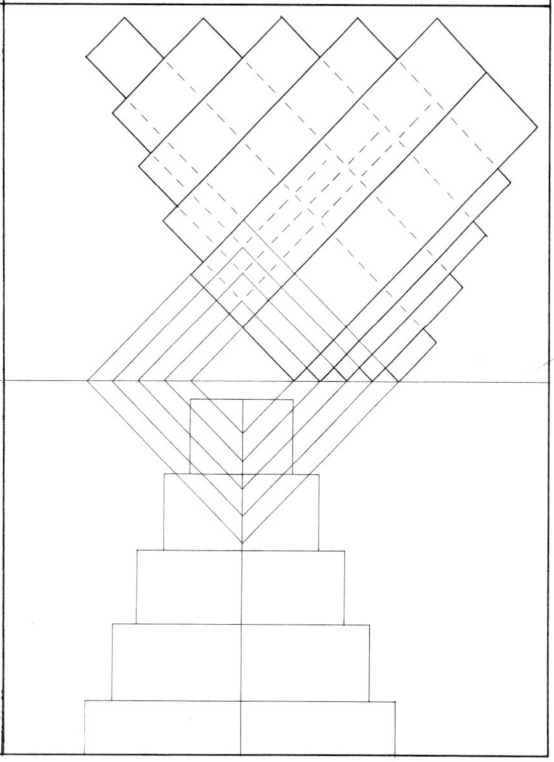

●建築シリーズ 2　Architecture series 2

71　**ワールドトレードセンター**　New York (1/2)　73　**尖塔**　Trans America (1/2)

74　**ピサの斜塔**　Leaning tower (1/2)　75　**バベルの塔**　Tower of Babel (1/2)

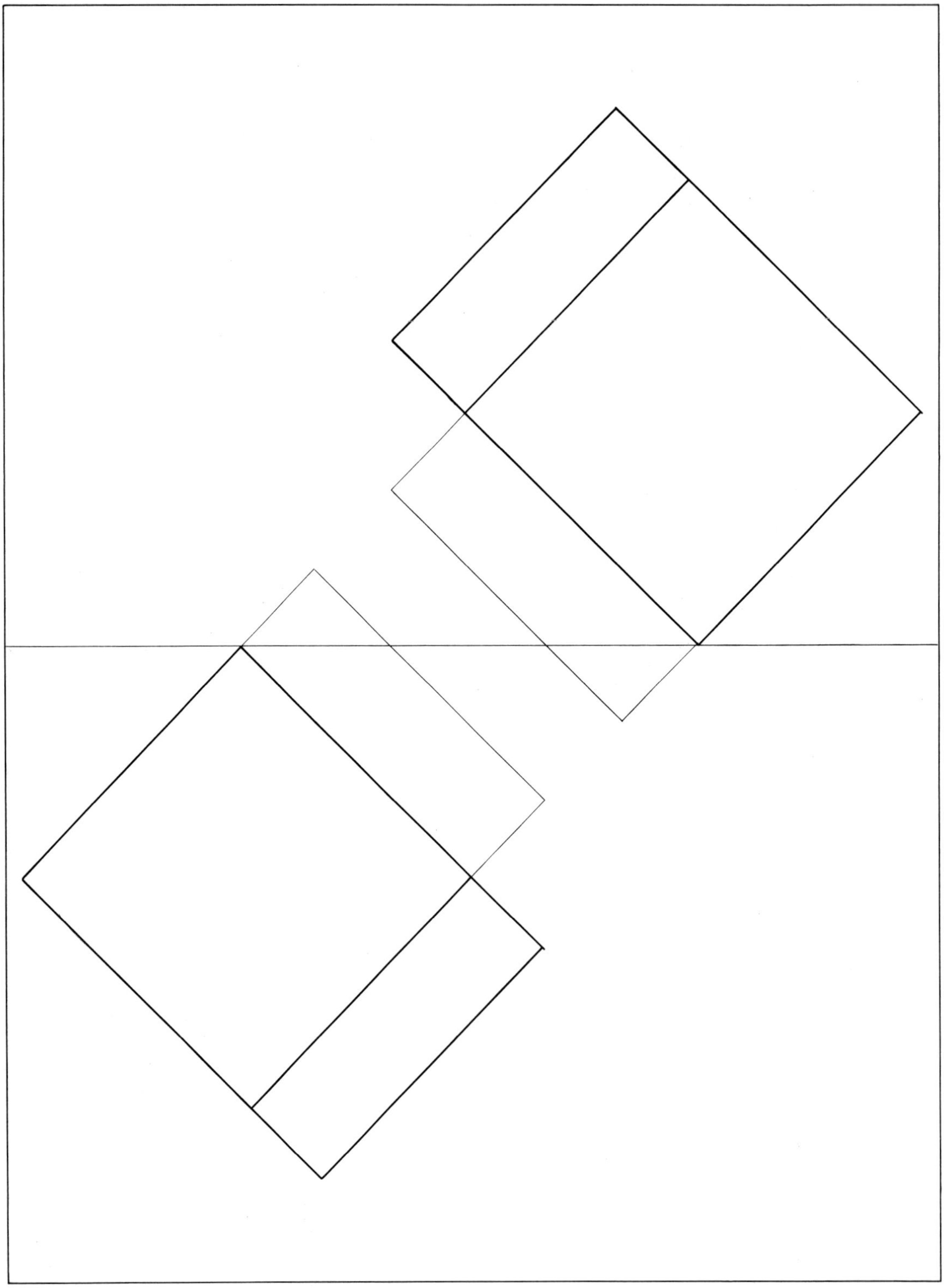

72 ツインタワー Twin tower (1/1)

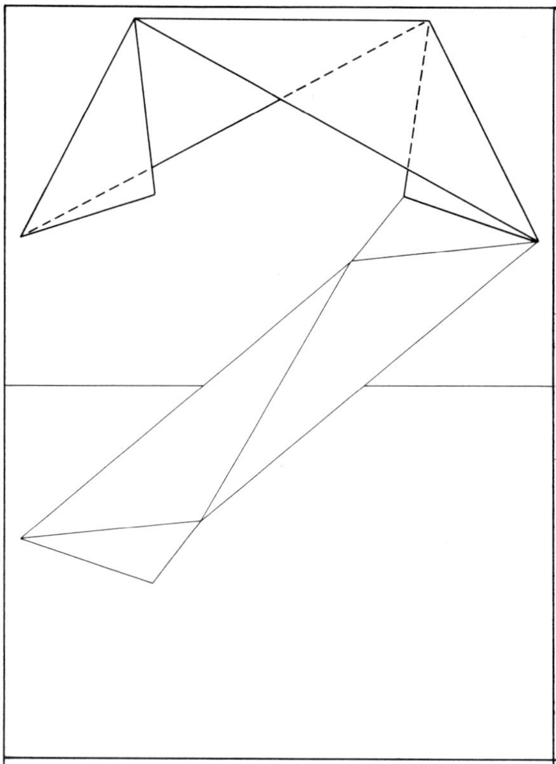

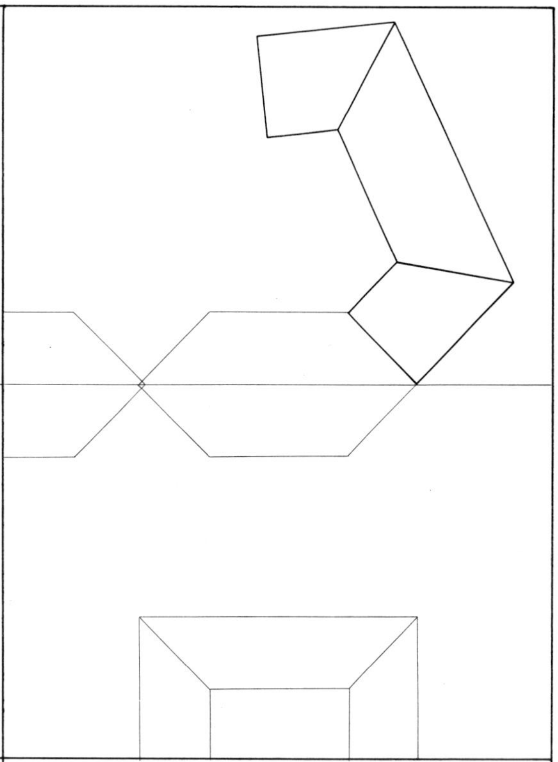

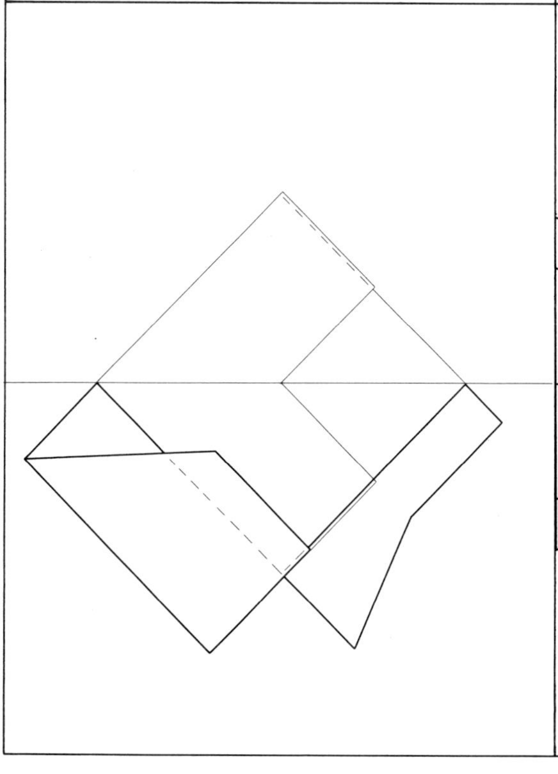

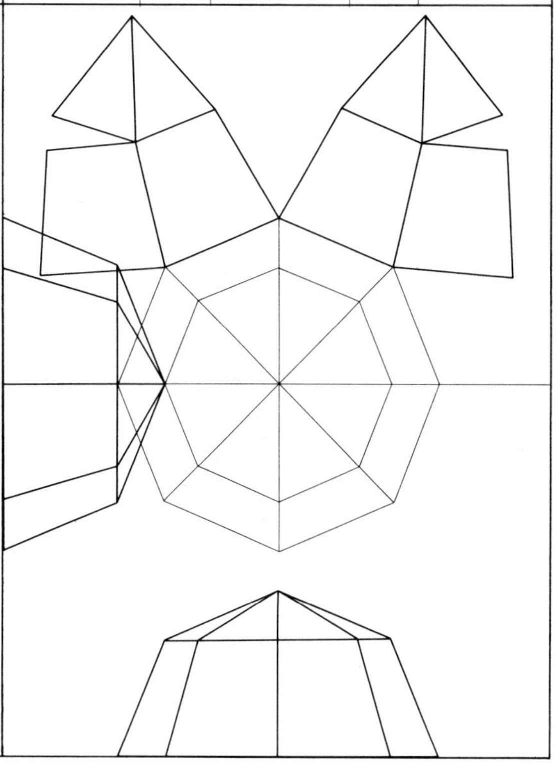

76 ブリッジ Bridge (1/2)

77 凱旋門 L'arc de Triomphe (1/2)

78 コートハウス Courtyard house (1/2)

79 包 Pao (1/2)

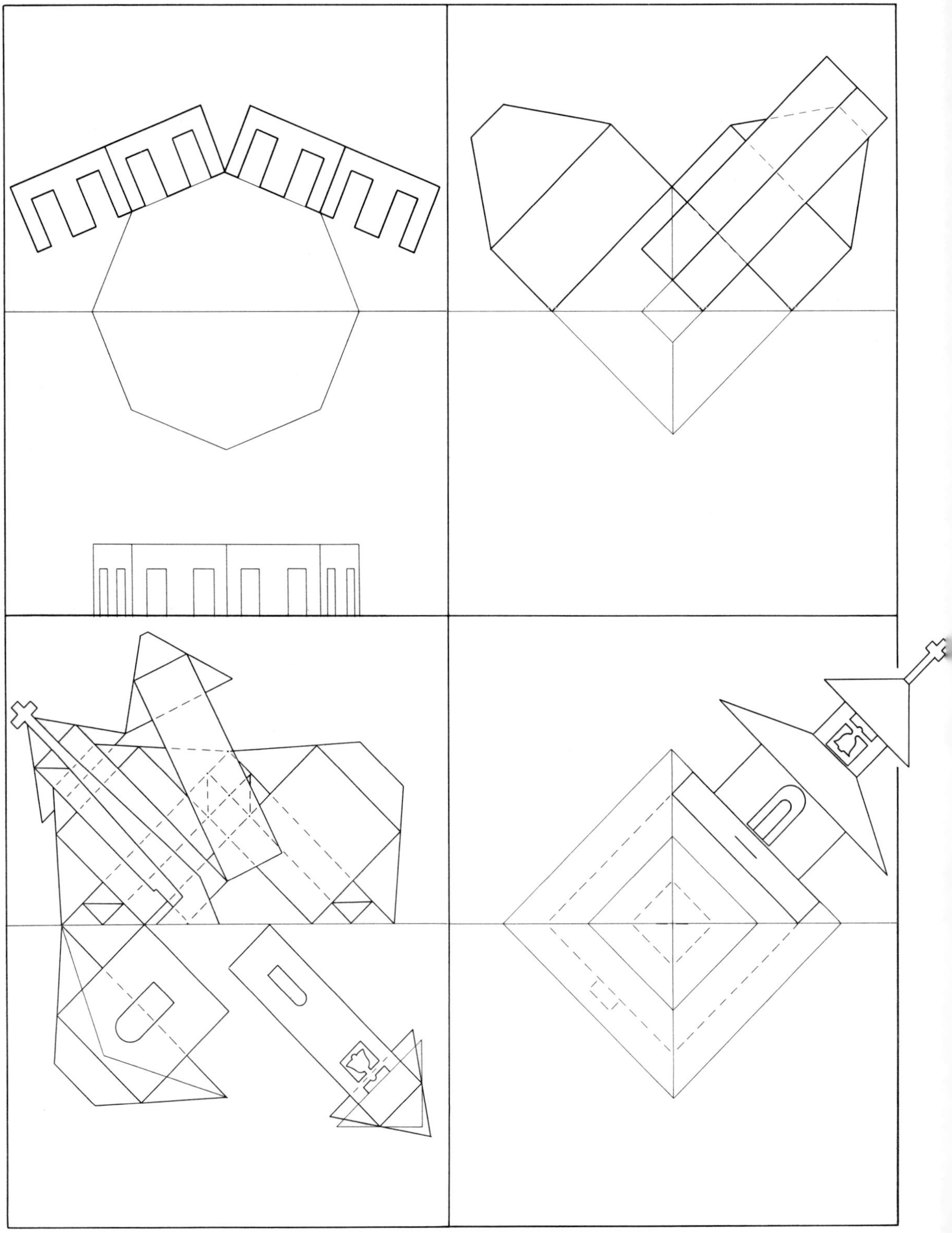

80　ストンヘンジ　Stonehenge (1/2)

81　サンタクロースの家　Chimney (1/2)

82　銀閣堂　Two storeyed (1/2)

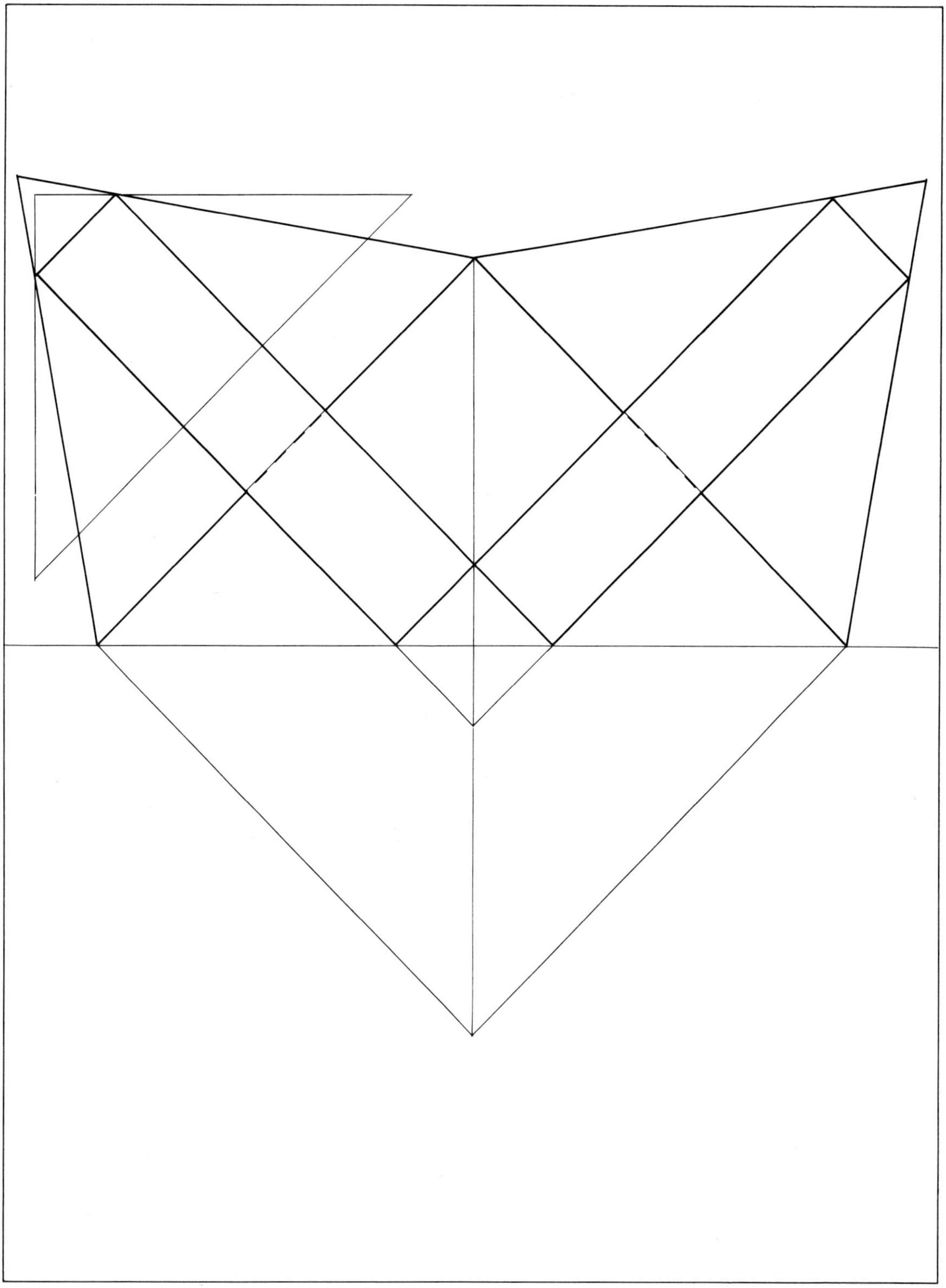

●屋根シリーズ　Roof series

83　傘堂　Umbrella（1/1）［奈良当麻寺北にある1本柱のお堂］

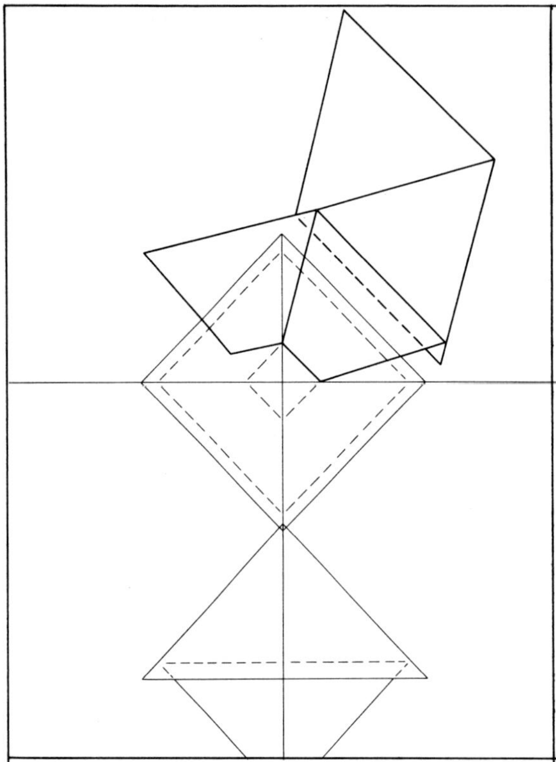

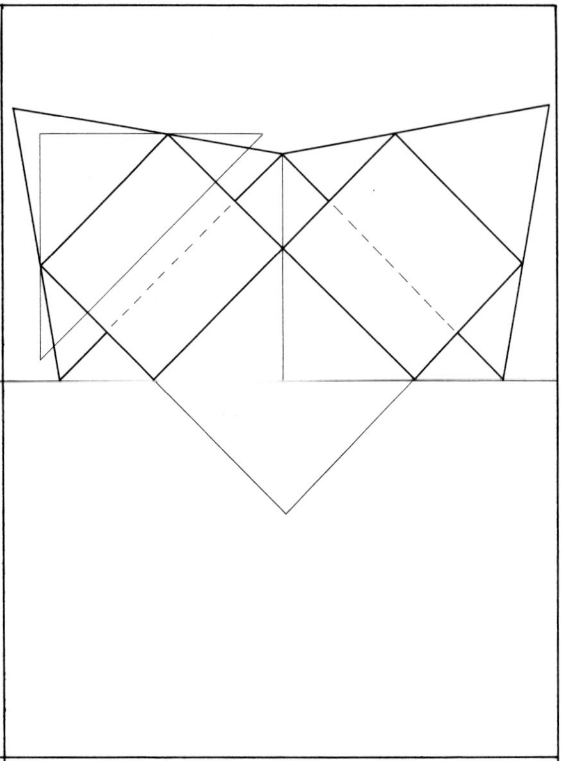

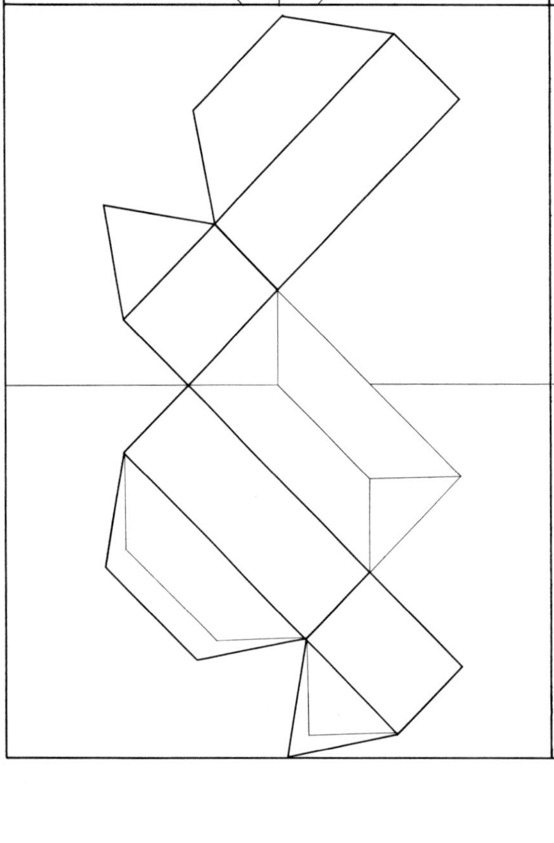

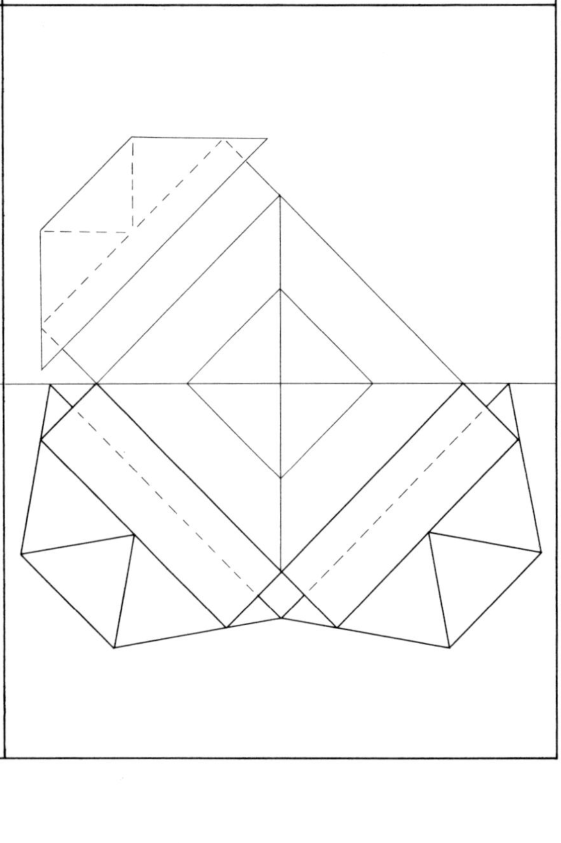

84 ヒュッテ Hütte (1/2)

85 方形 Pyramidal (1/2)

86 寄棟 Hipped roof (1/2)

87 くど造り Funnel (1/2) [佐賀県有明海近くの民家]

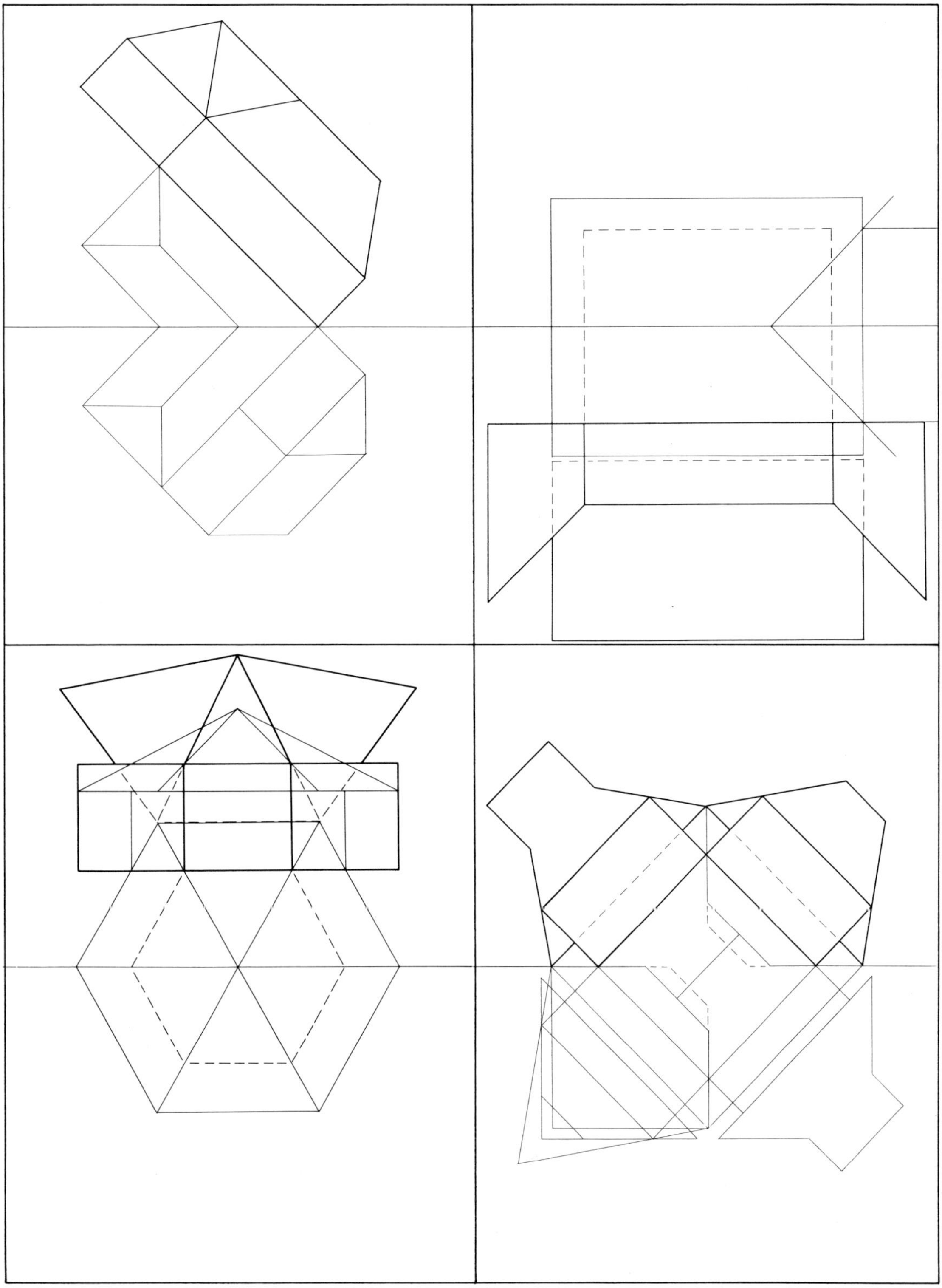

88 **曲り屋** L-shaped (1/2)

89 **切妻** Gabled (1/2)

90 **六角堂** Hexagon (1/2)

91 **入母屋** Hipped gable (1/2)

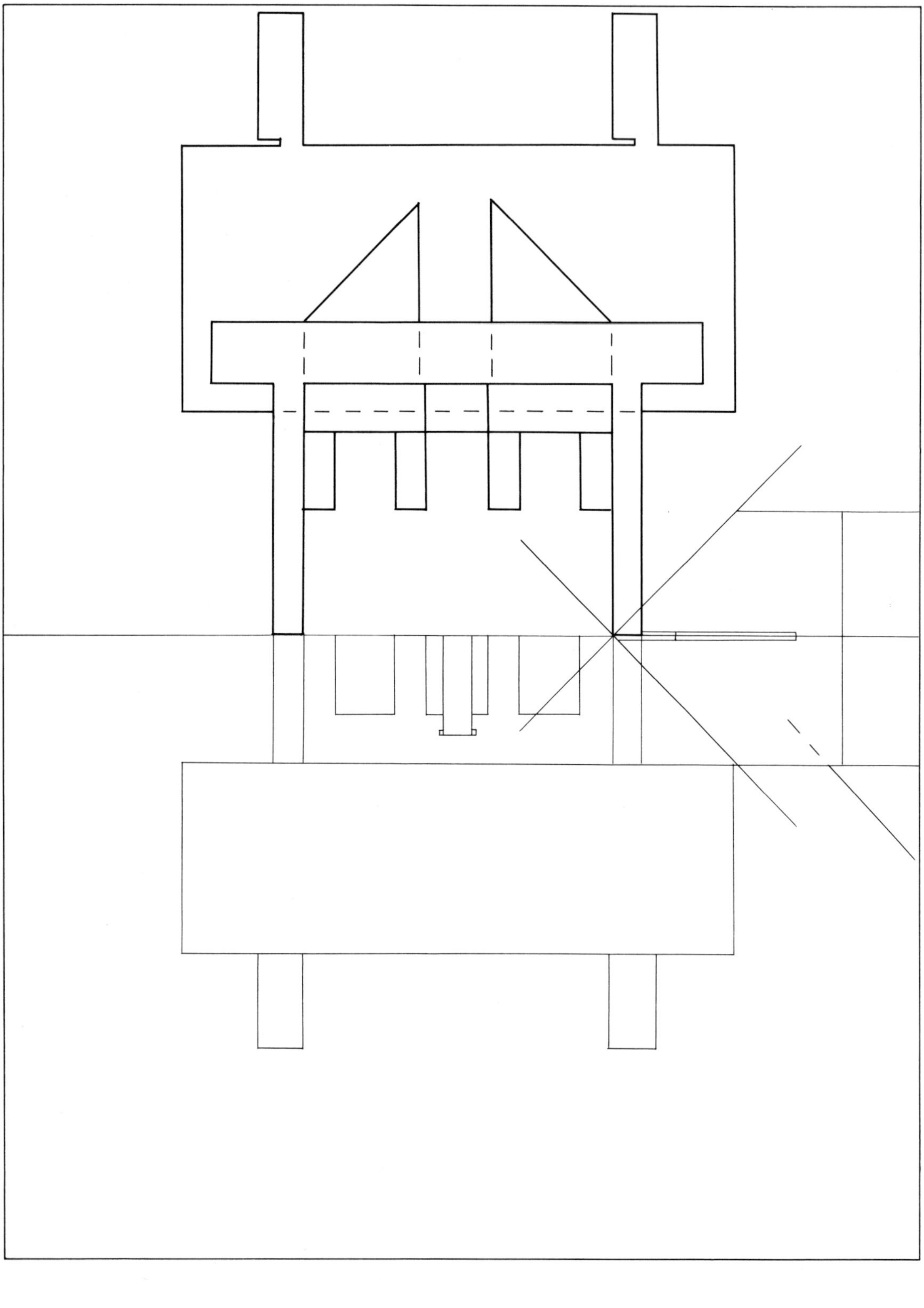

92　お伊勢さん　Ise shrine (1/1)

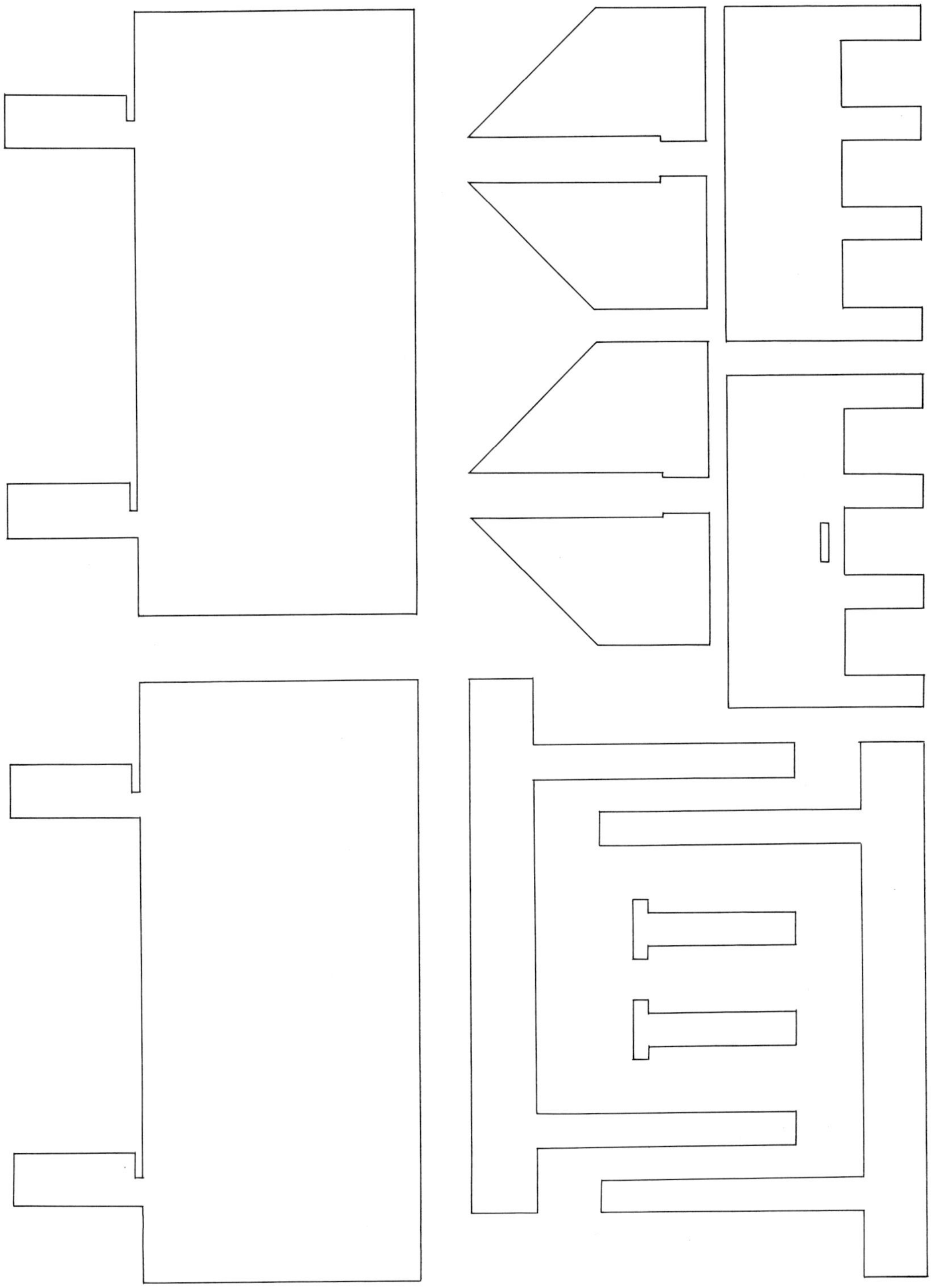

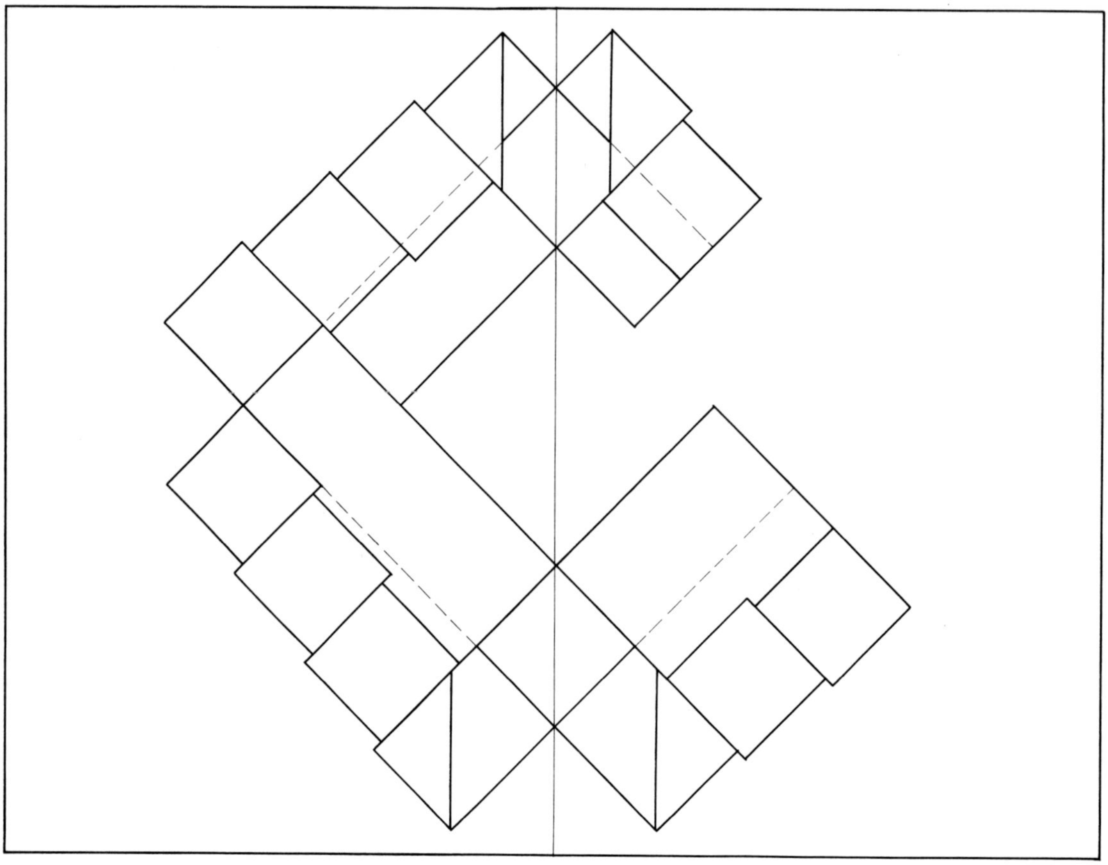

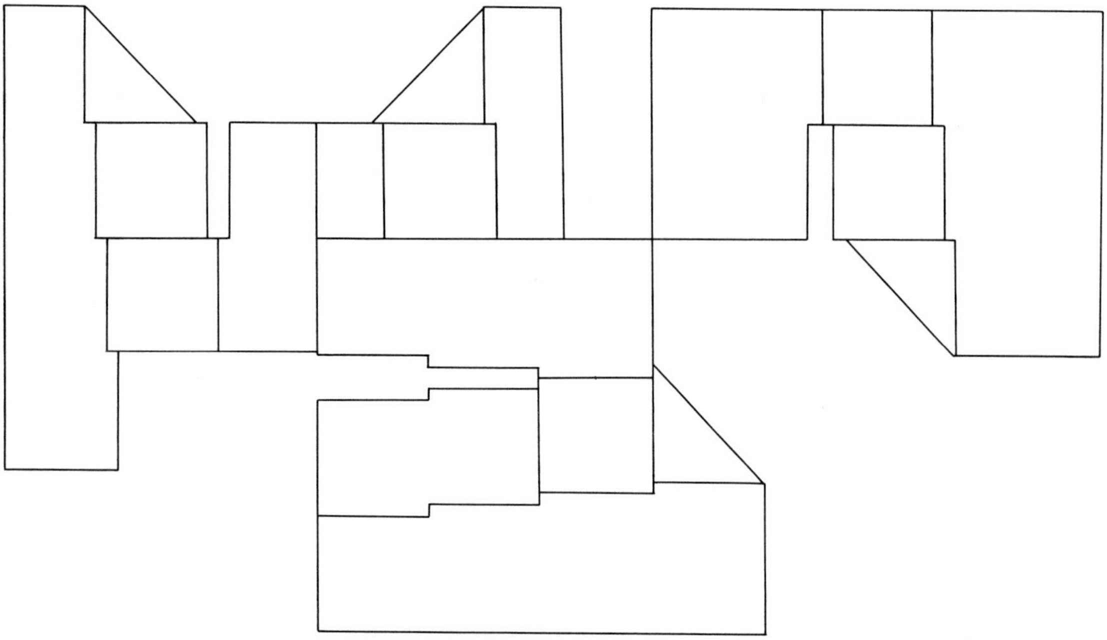

● ペンローズ シリーズ　**Penrose series**

93　ペンローズの階段　Penrose stair (3/4)

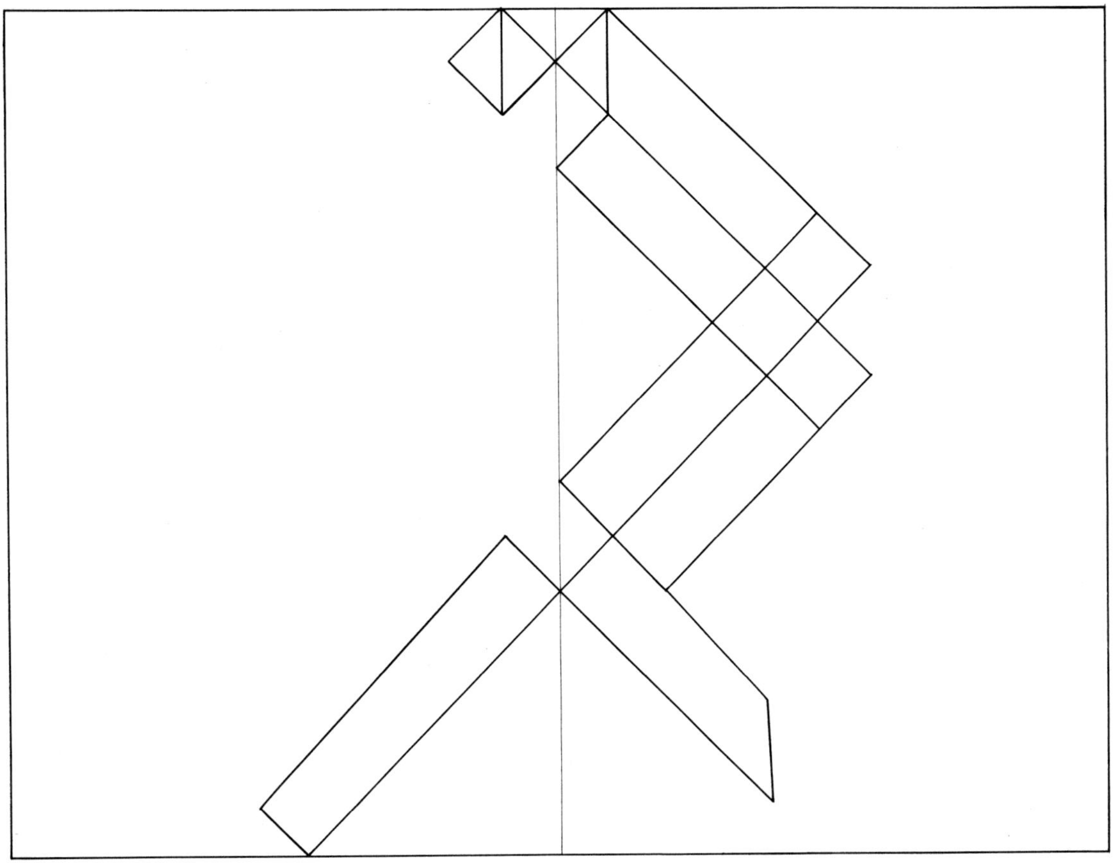

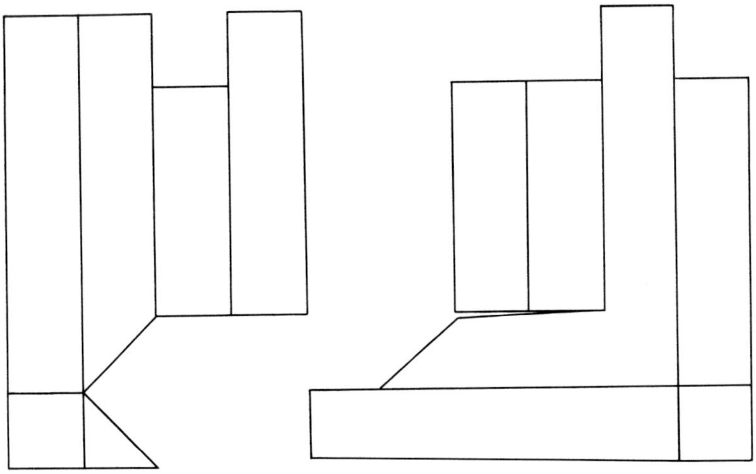

94　ペンローズの三角形　Penrose triangle (3/4)

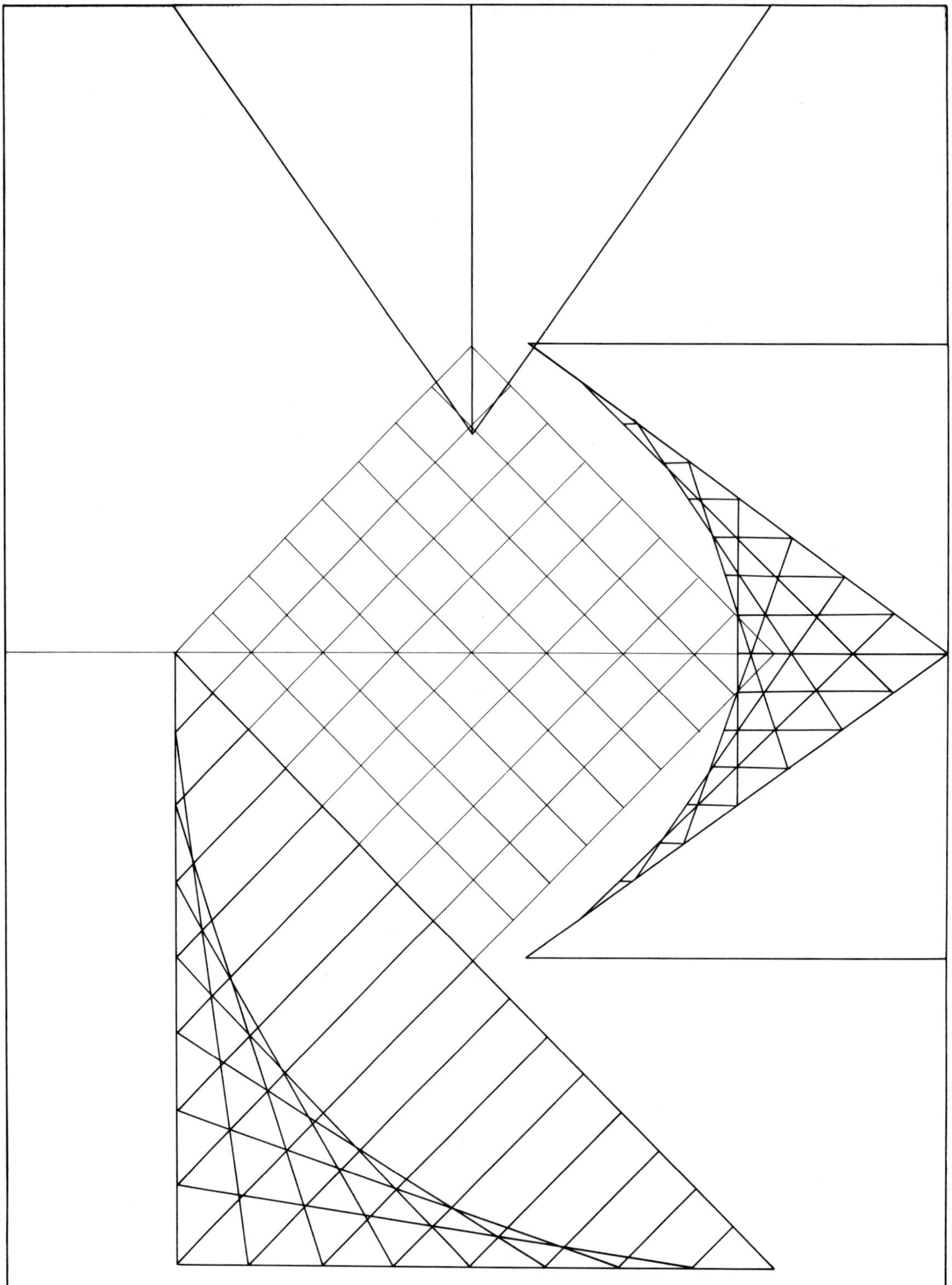

● 線体シリーズ　Linearoid series

95　H.P.シェル　Hyperbolic Paraboloid 1 （1/1）

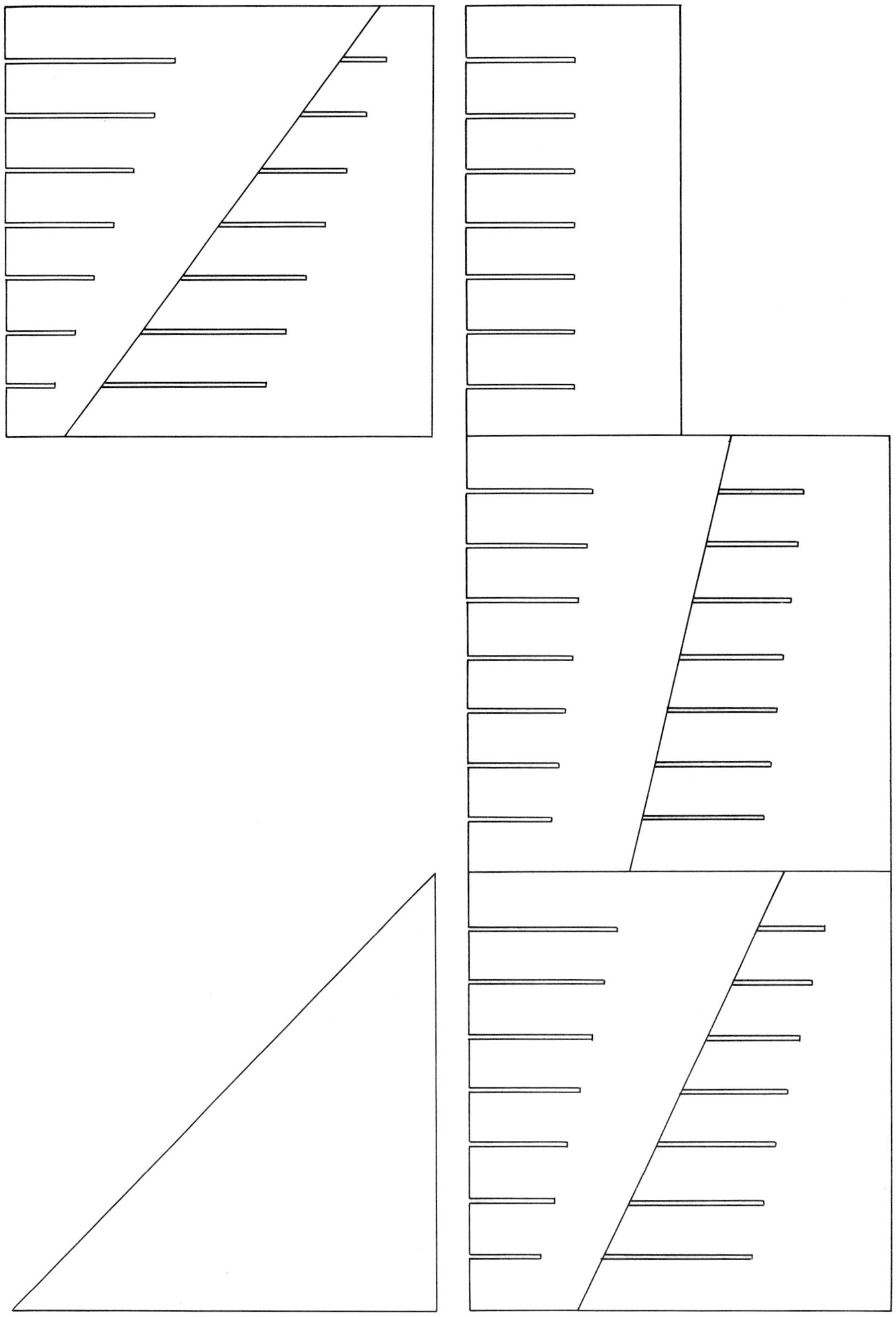

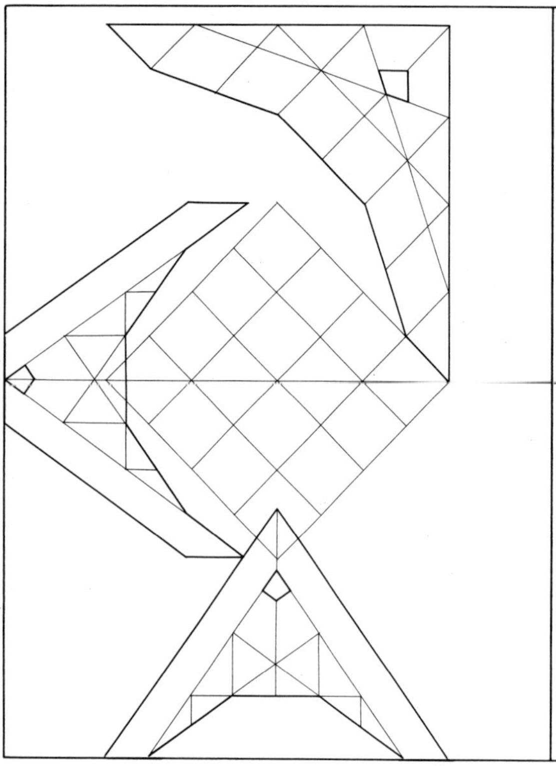

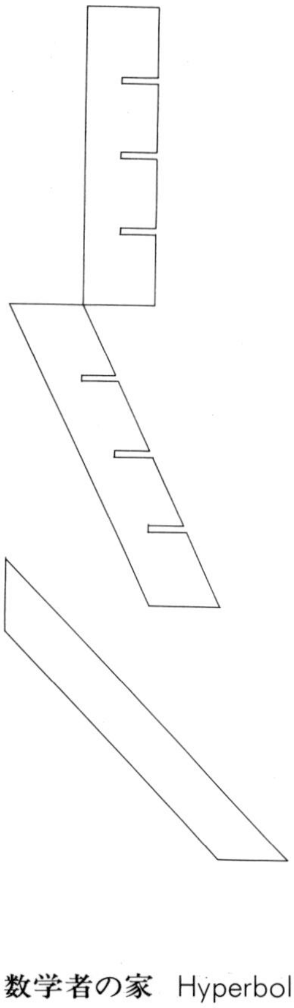

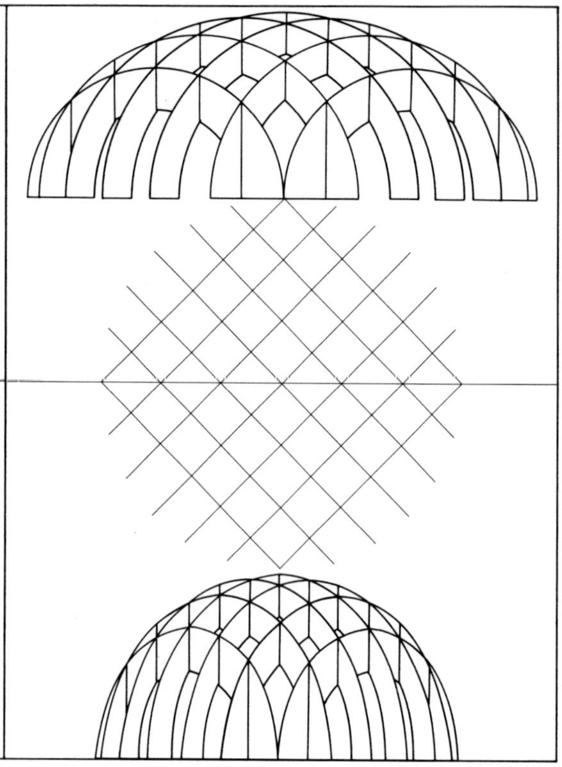

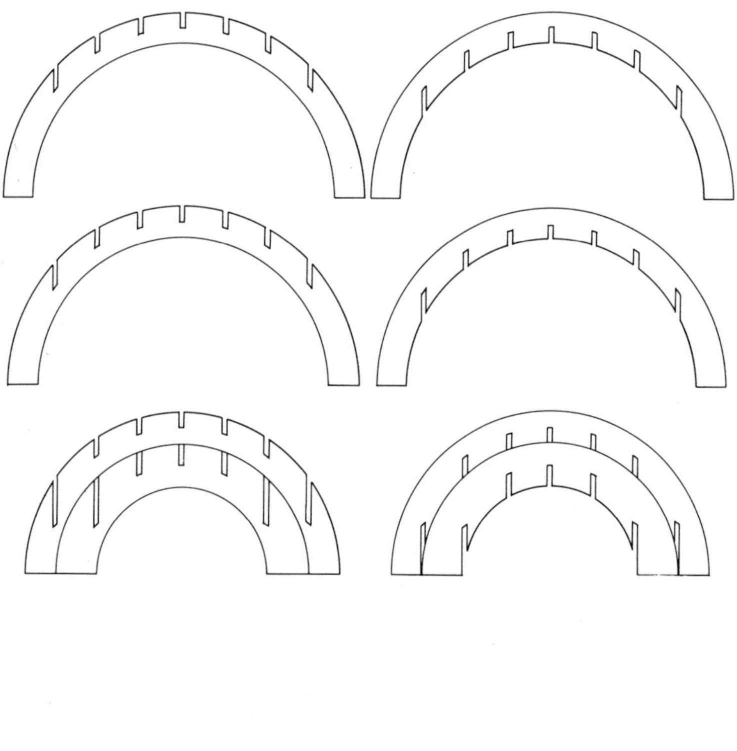

96　数学者の家　Hyperbolic Paraboloid 2 (1/2)　　97　半球　Hemisphere 7 (1/2)

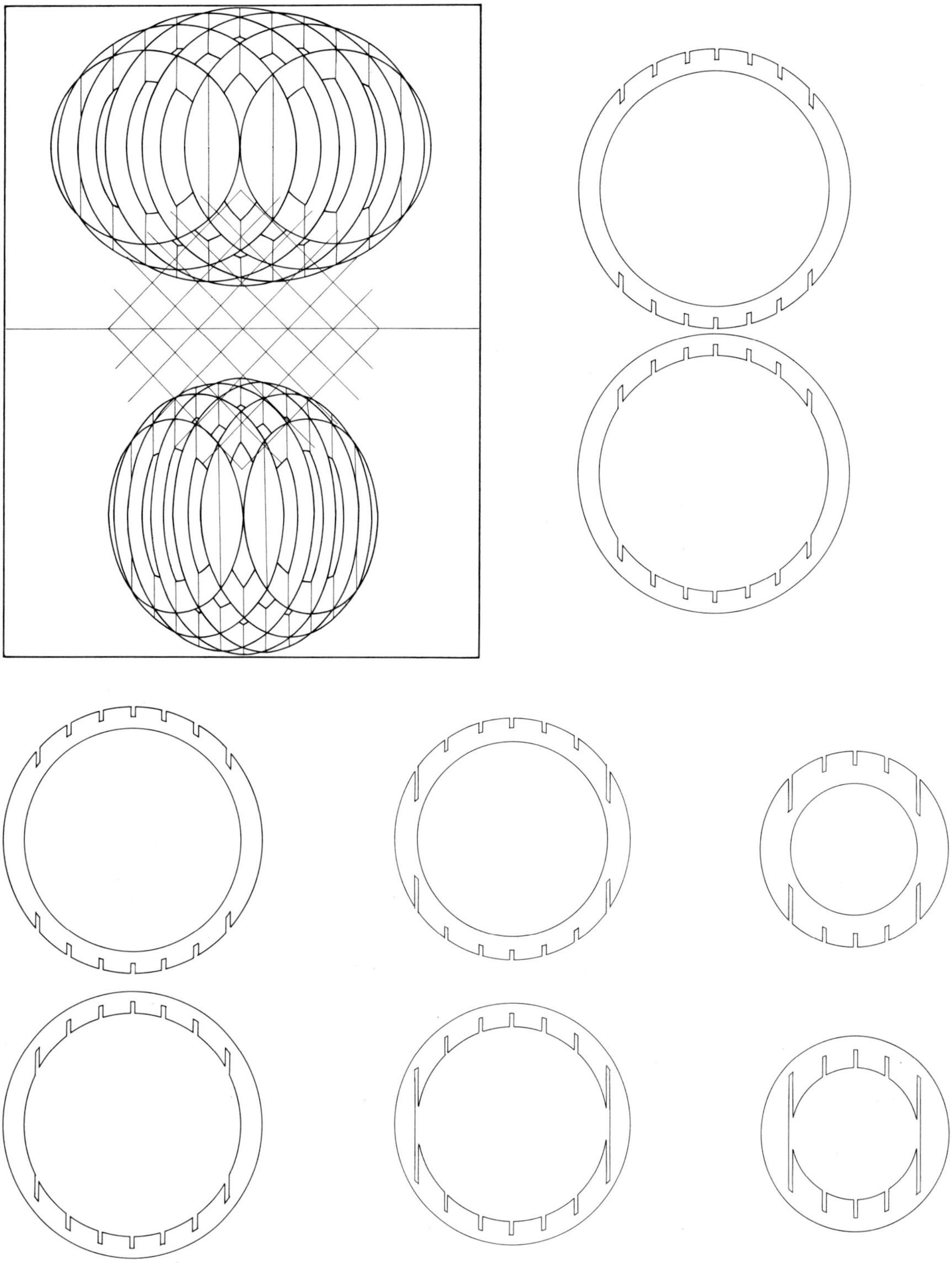

98 球 Sphere (1/2)

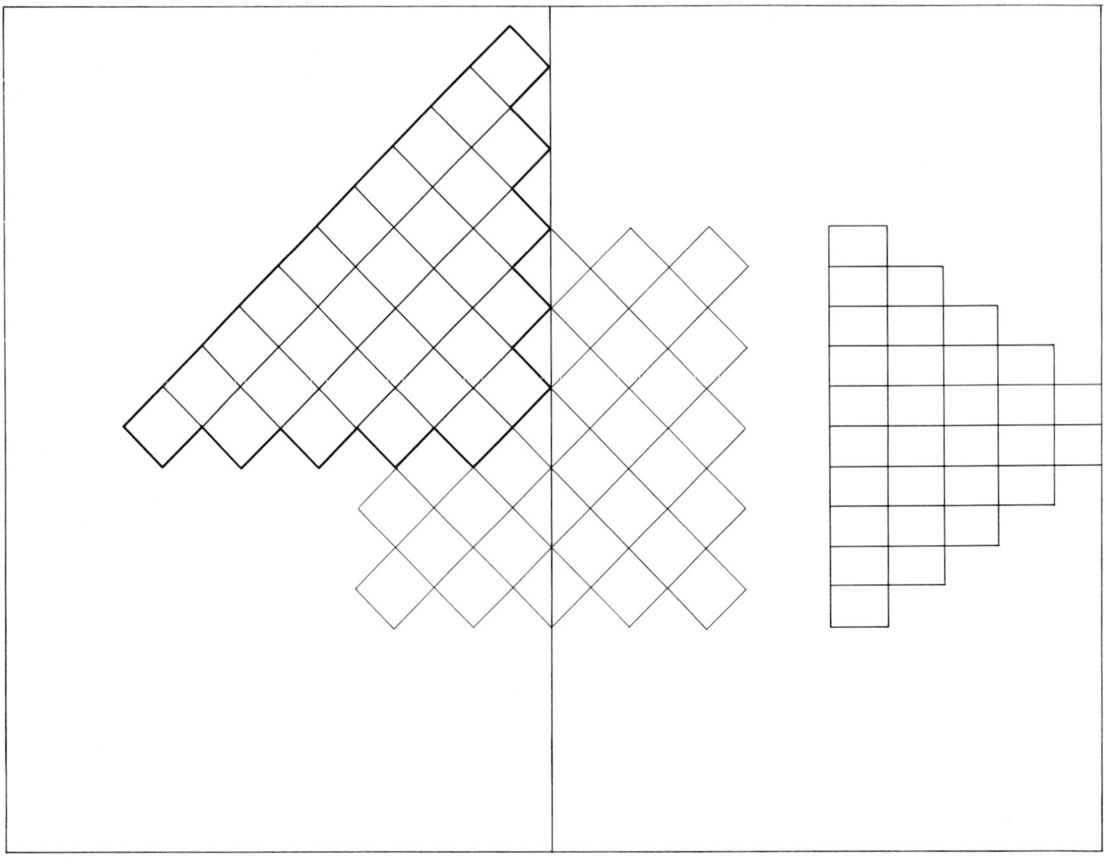

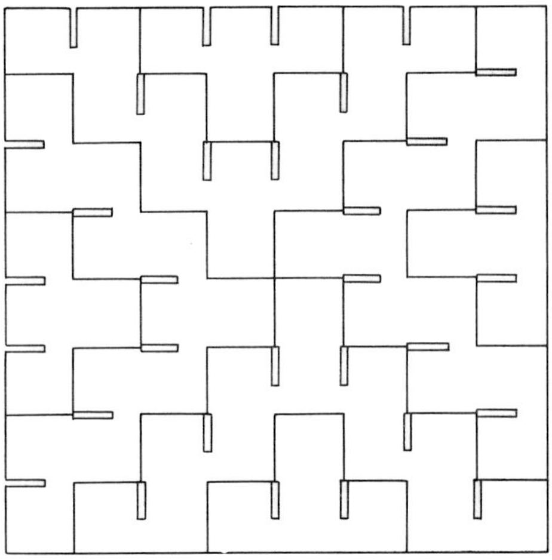

99　スイスの樹　Alpine tree (3/4)

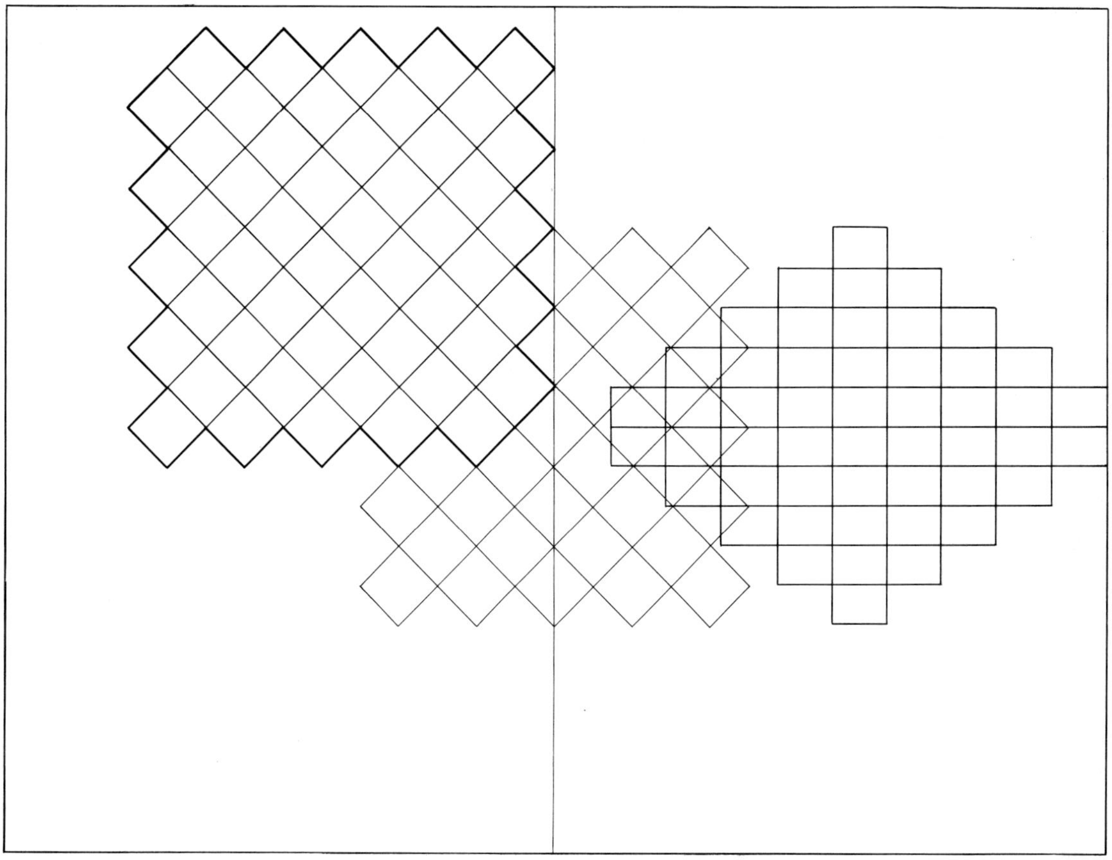

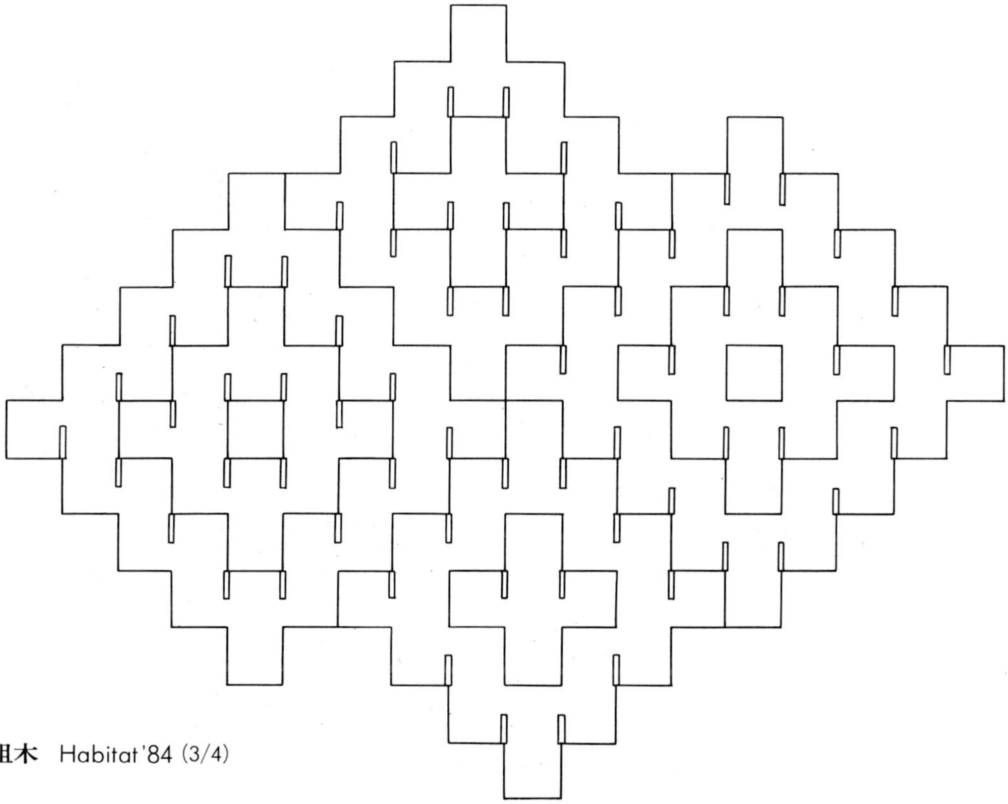

100　組木　Habitat'84 (3/4)

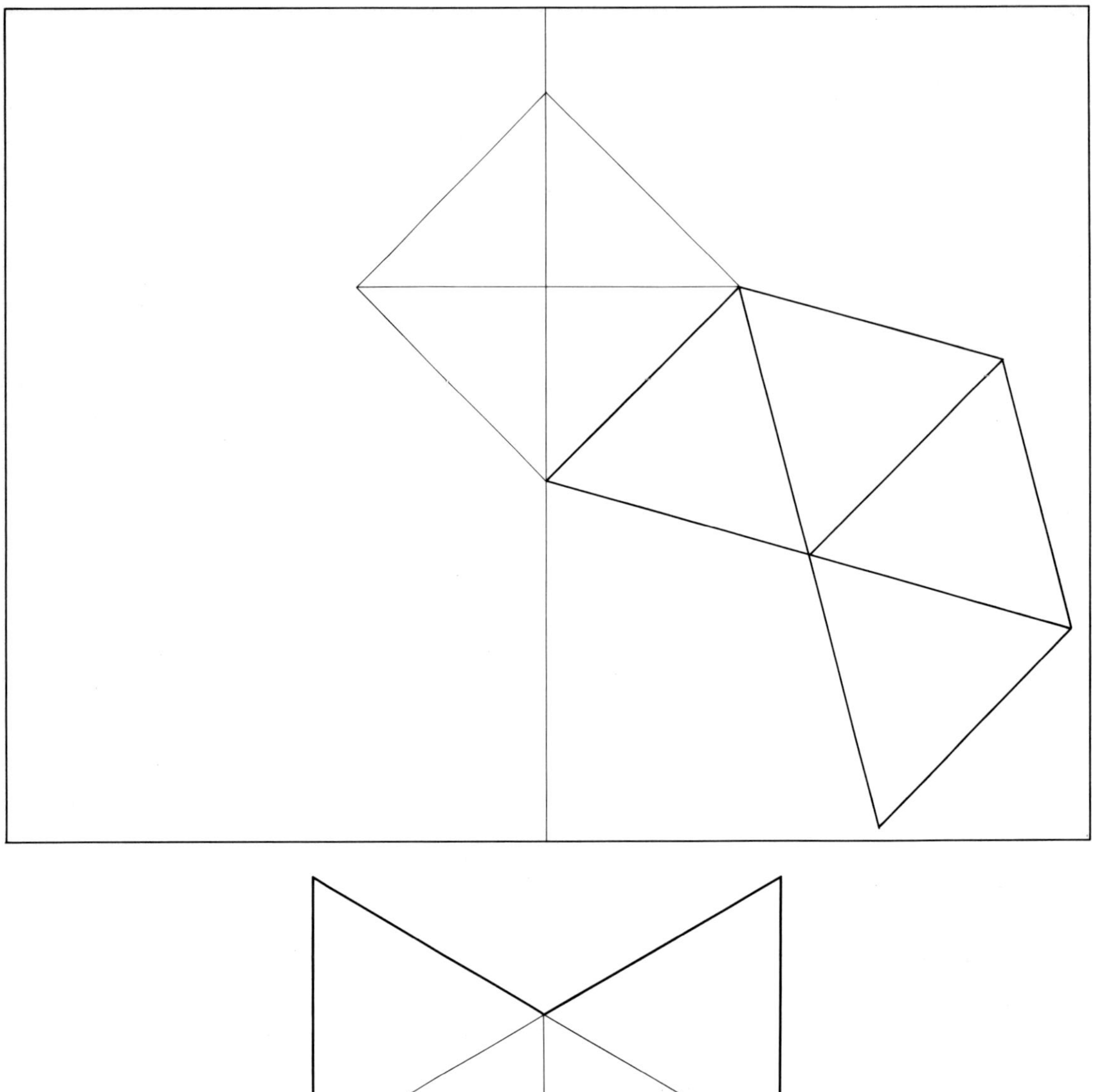

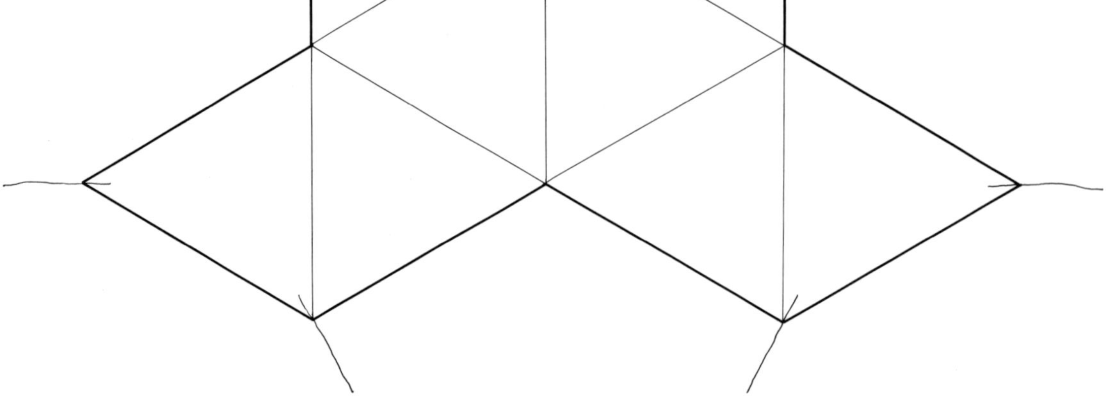

●完全立体シリーズ　Holohedra series

101　正八面体　Octahedron (3/4)

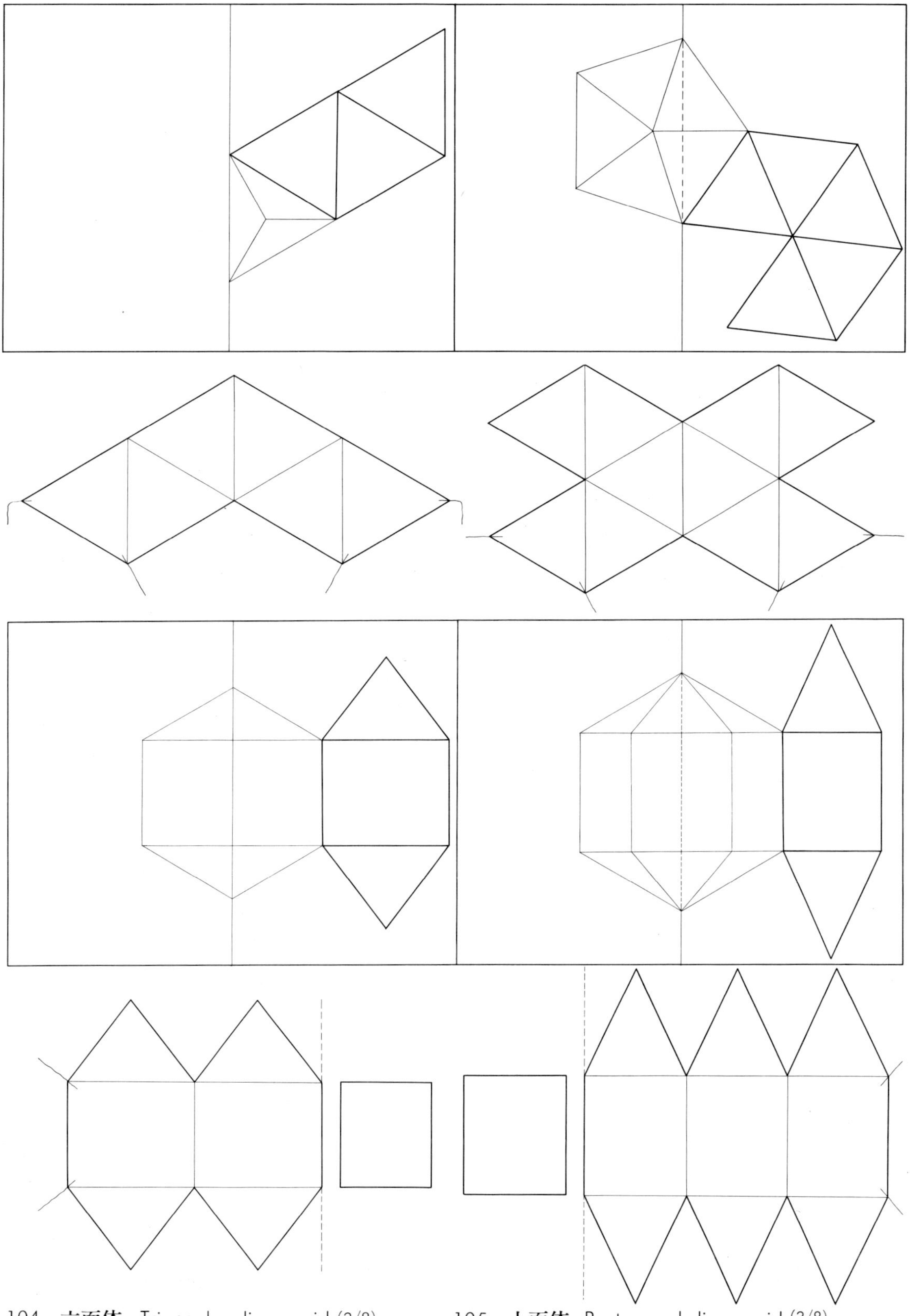

104　**六面体**　Triangular di-pyramid (3/8)

103　**十二面体**　Dodecahedron (3/8)

105　**十面体**　Pentagonal di-pyramid (3/8)

102　**十八面体**　Octadecahedron (3/8)

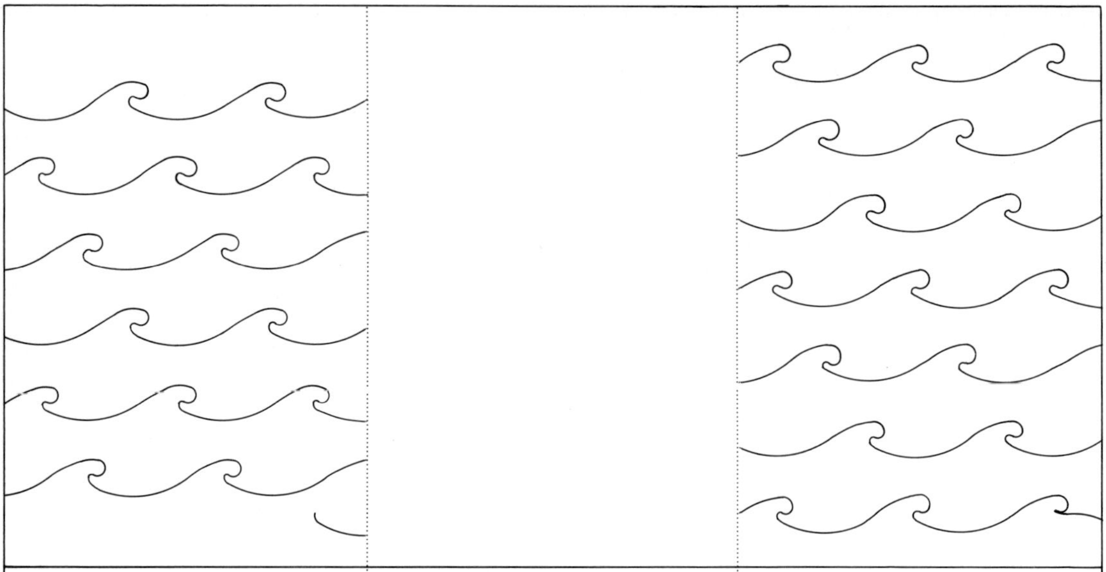

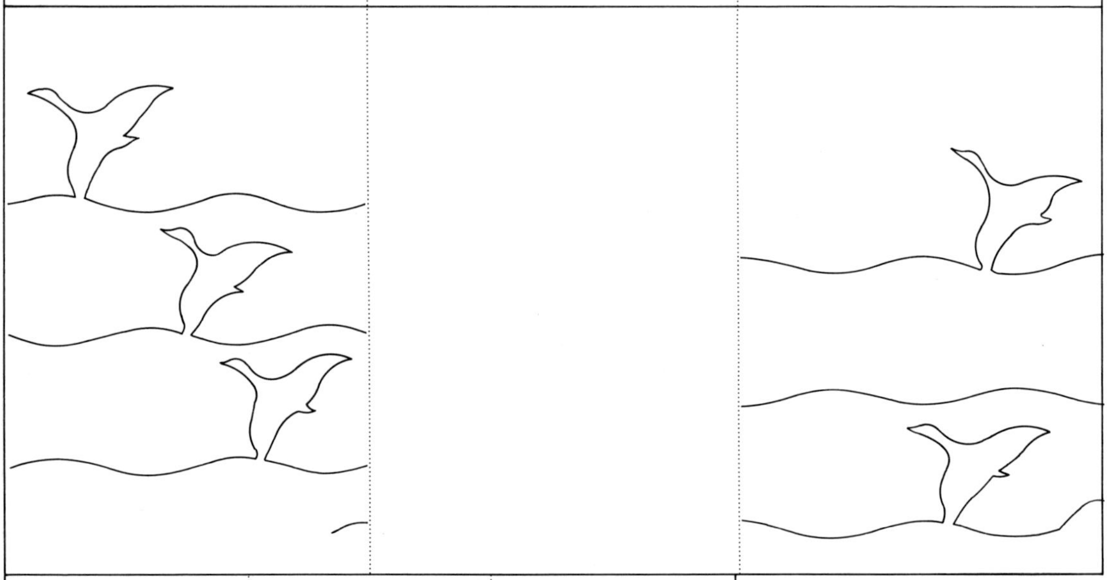

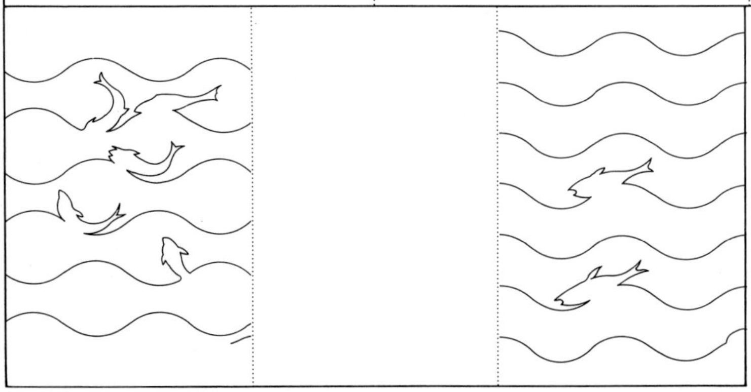

106～108

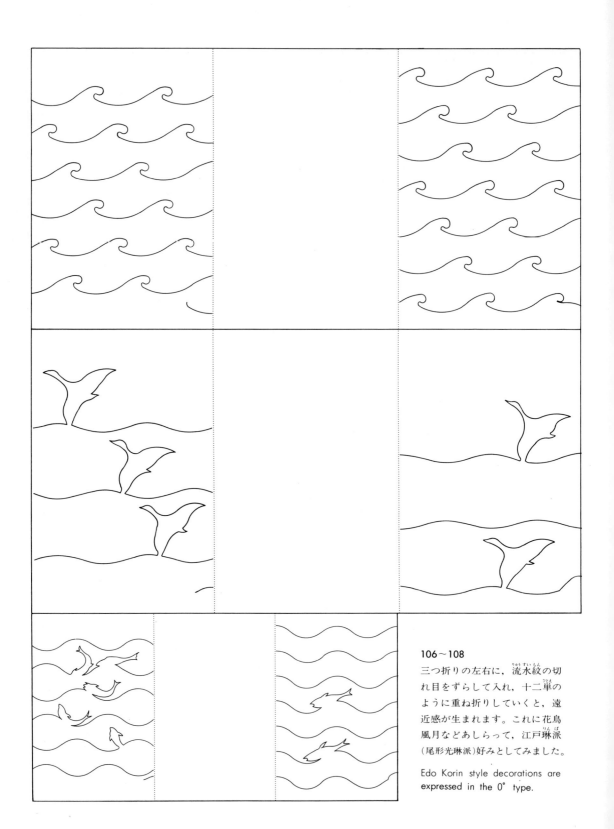

三つ折りの左右に，流水紋の切れ目をずらして入れ，十二単のように重ね折りしていくと，遠近感が生まれます。これに花鳥風月などあしらって，江戸琳派（尾形光琳派）好みとしてみました。

Edo Korin style decorations are expressed in the 0° type.

●平面シリーズ　Plain series

106　**荒磯**　Reefy shore (1/2)

107　**いそしぎ**　Flyway (1/2)

108　**たわむれのコイ**　Dancing carp (1/3)

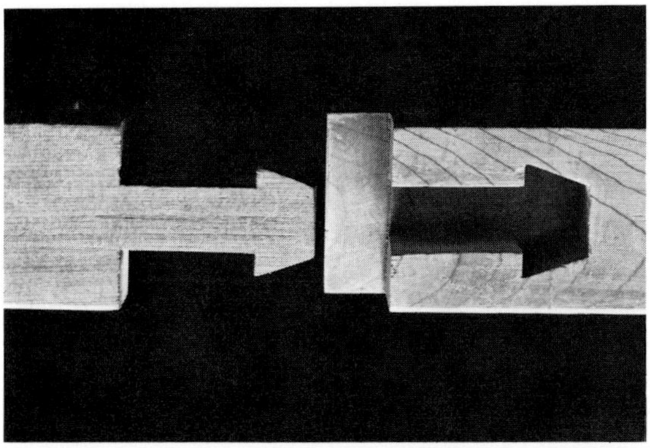

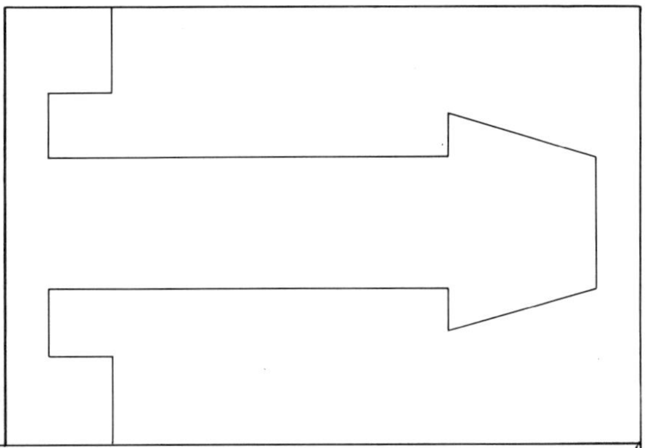

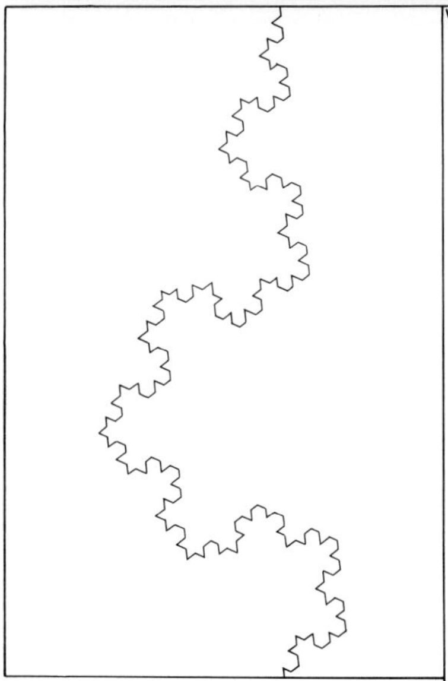

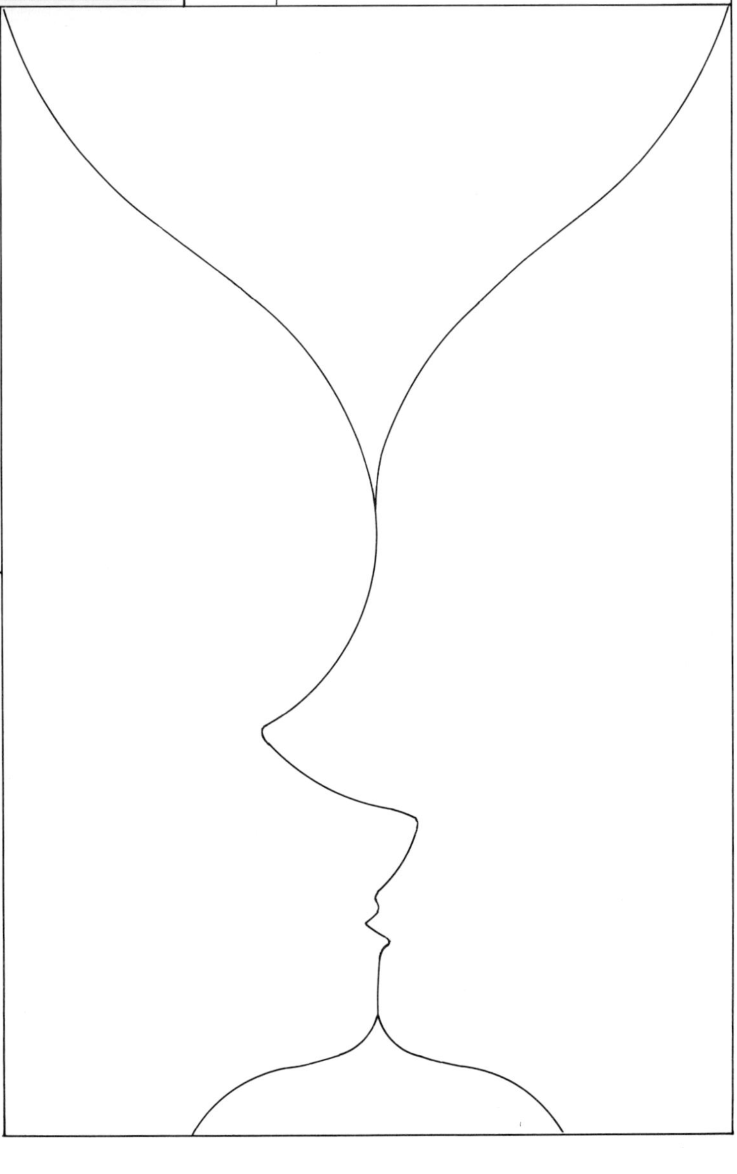

109～111

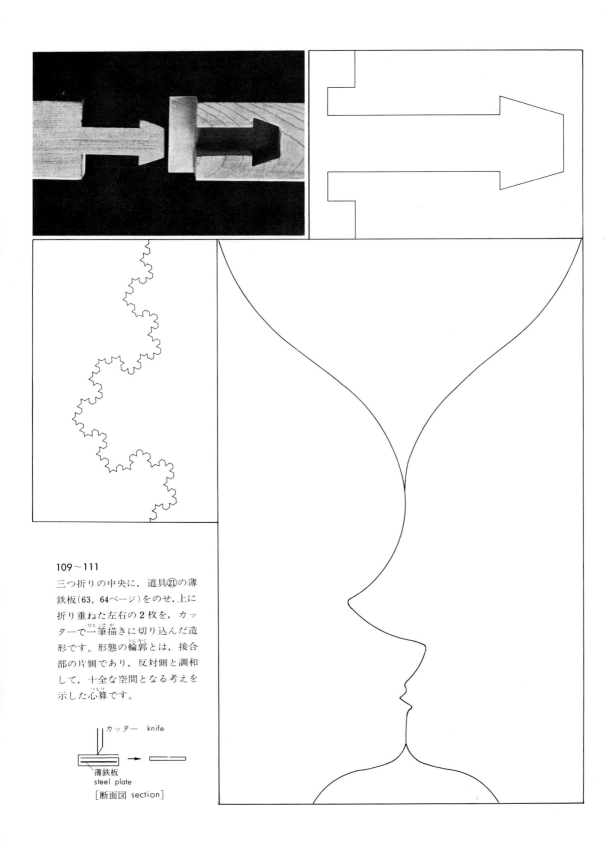

三つ折りの中央に，道具㉑の薄鉄板（63，64ページ）をのせ，上に折り重ねた左右の２枚を，カッターで一筆描きに切り込んだ造形です。形態の輪郭とは，接合部の片側であり，反対側と調和して，十全な空間となる考えを示した心算です。

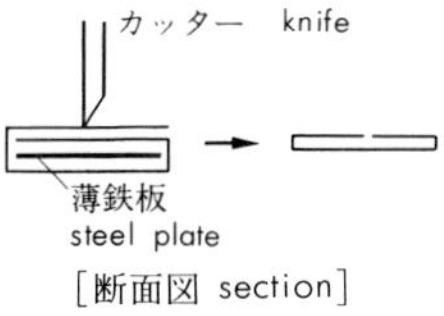

109 **分割** Fractal (1/2)

110 **鎌継** Mortise and tenon joint (1/2)

111 **愛** Love (1/1)

kami waza

紙 技 !

A very gifted art!

著者略歴

茶谷正洋（ちゃたに まさひろ）

1934年	広島に生まれる
1952年	日比谷高校卒業
1956年	東京工業大学卒業
同　年	大成建設設計部
1961年	建設省建築研究所
1967年	工学博士
1969年	東京工業大学助教授
1977年	ワシントン大学客員助教授
1980年	東京工業大学教授　現在に至る
1981年	日本建築家協会理事
1983年	日本建築学会理事，同編集委員長

オリガミック・アーキテクチャー展

1982年	銀座松屋デザインギャラリー
1983年	青山自在堂
	静岡ガスサロン
	西友（吉祥寺，高針，諫早）
	早稲田画廊
	池袋西武ハビタギャラリー

折り紙建築　　**定価 1,400円**

昭和58年12月20日　第1版 発　行
昭和58年12月25日　第1版 第2刷
昭和59年1月20日　第1版 第3刷
昭和59年2月25日　第1版 第4刷
昭和59年3月20日　第1版 第5刷
昭和59年4月30日　第1版 第6刷
昭和59年7月20日　第1版 第7刷
昭和59年9月20日　第1版 第8刷

著作権者との協定により検印廃止

著　者　茶　谷　正　洋
発行者　山　本　泰　四　郎
発行所　株式会社 **彰　国　社**
160 東京都新宿区坂町25
電　話　359－3231（大代表）
振替口座　東　京　6－173401

自然科学書協会会員
工学書協会会員

Printed in Japan

装幀・長谷川純雄　製版・近藤写真製版所　印刷・清和印刷　製本・昇栄社

ISBN4-395-27011-5　C3072

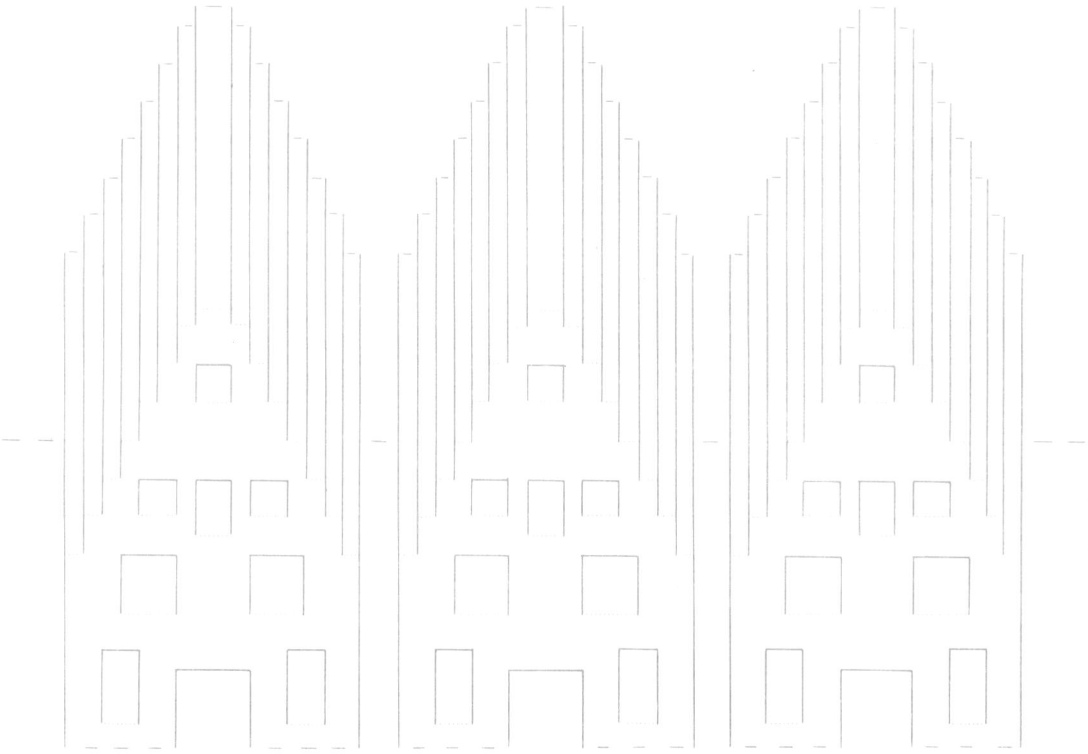

22 アムステルダム Amsterdam façade

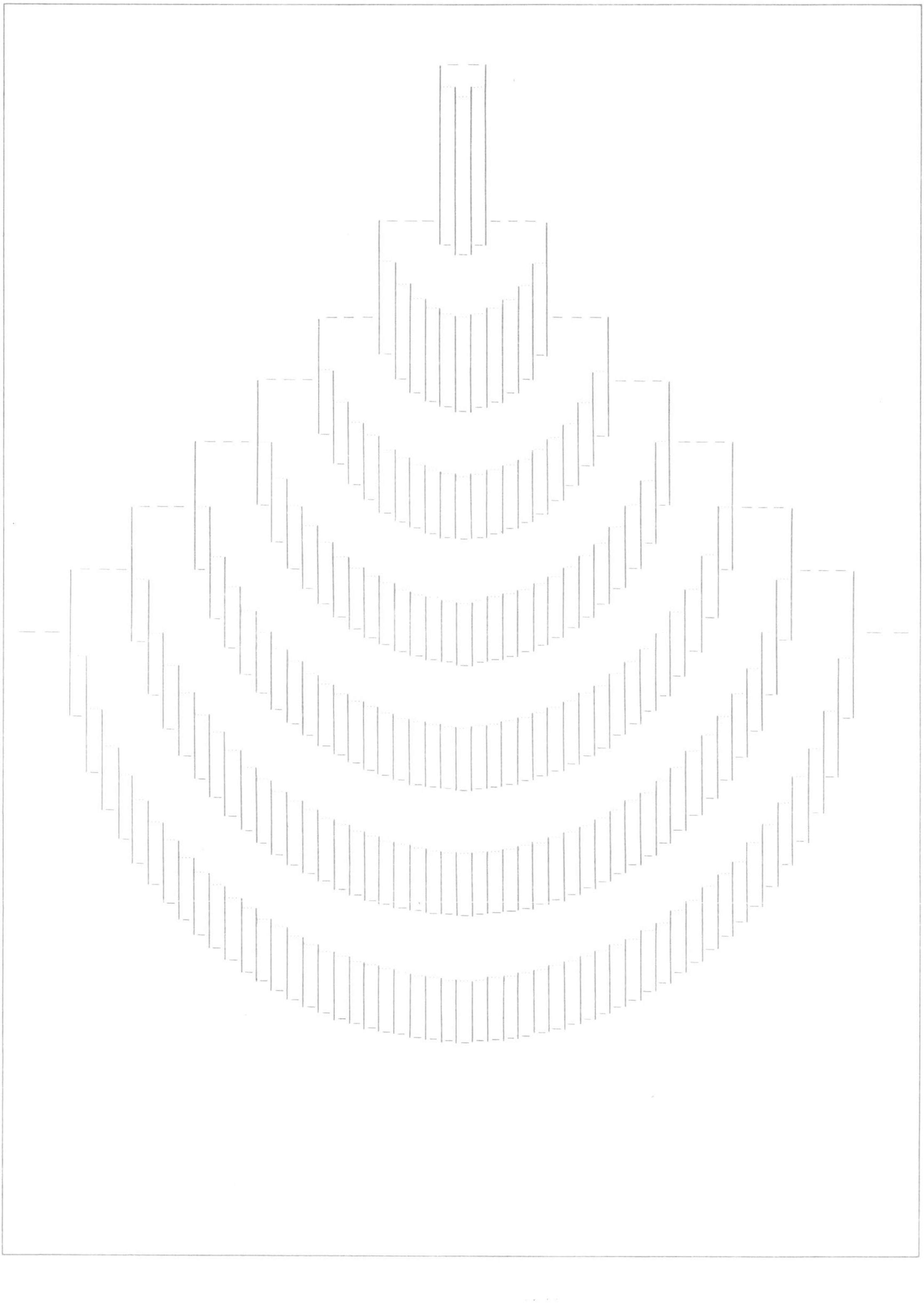

26 ウェディングパレス Wedding palace

51 Good luck 2

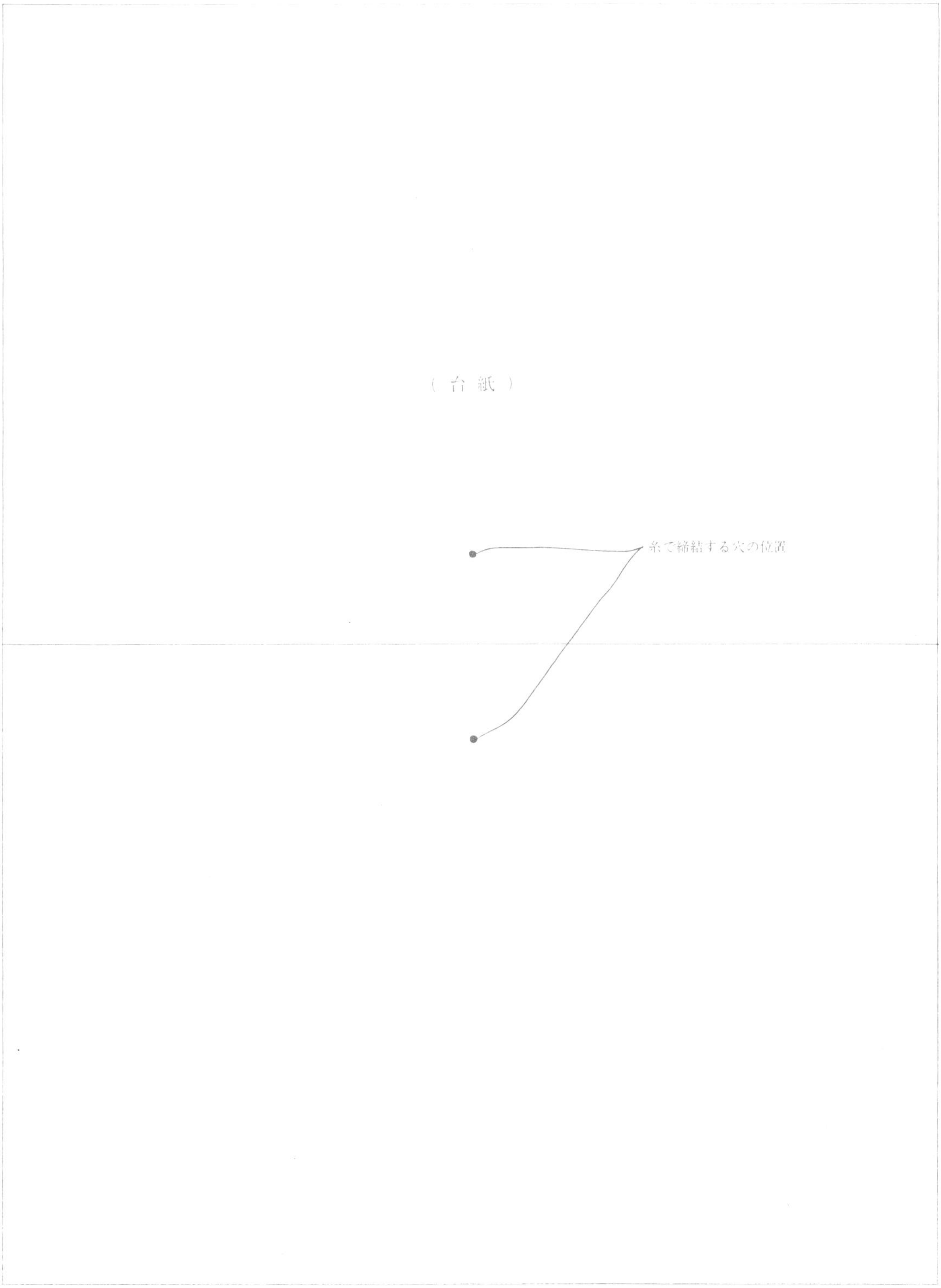

128ページのような各パーツを作り，型紙に２コと書いてあるものは紙を重ねて切り，組合せた上で67ページ③④のように別にこの大きさの台紙に締結する。

98 球 Sphere

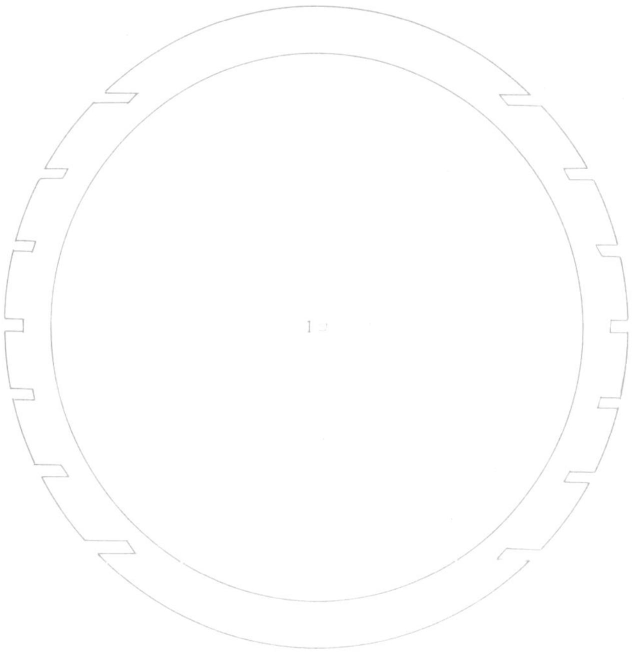
1コ

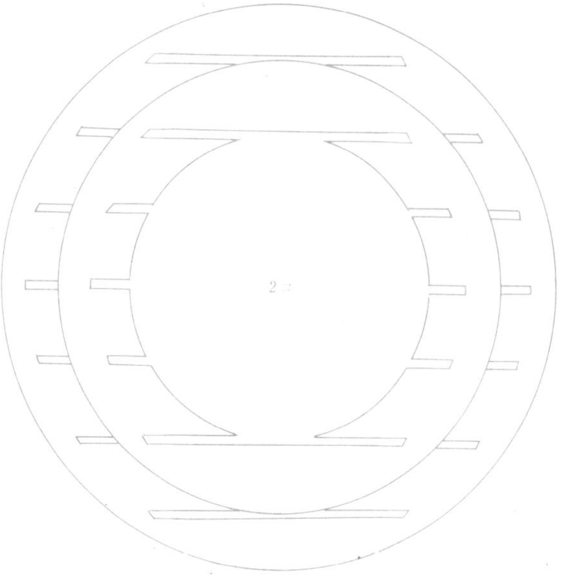
2コ

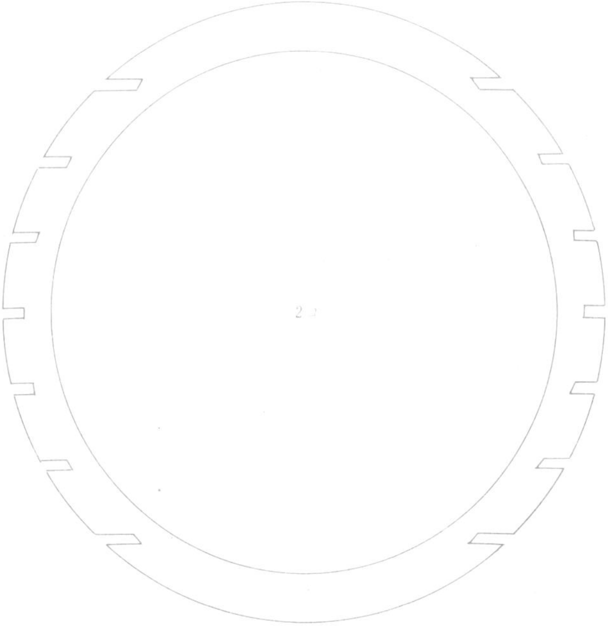
2コ

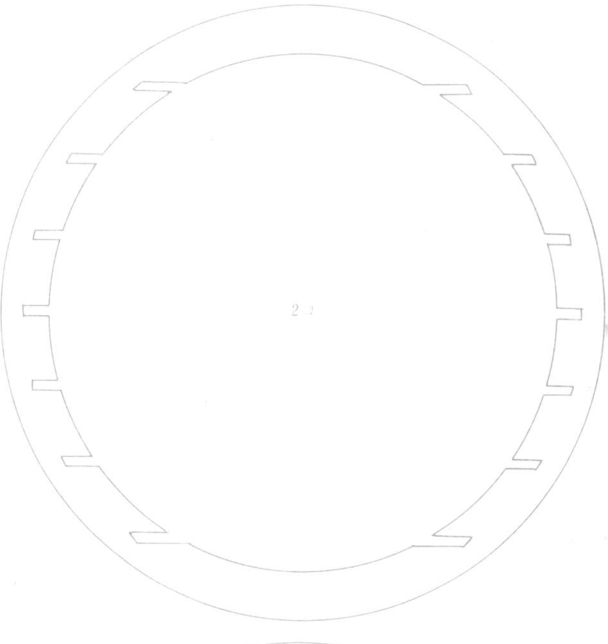
2コ

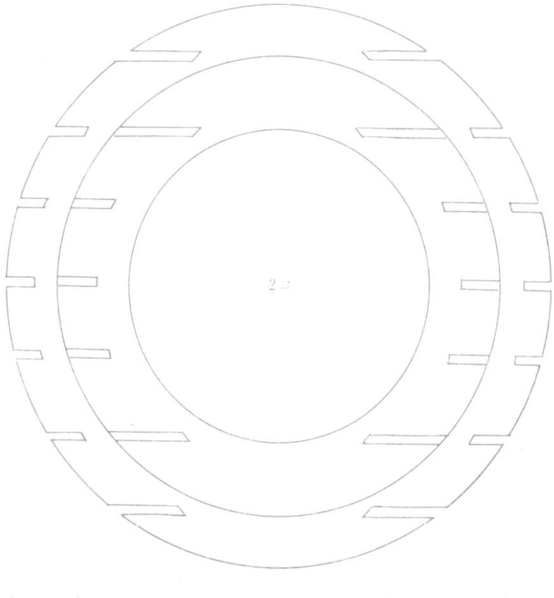
2コ

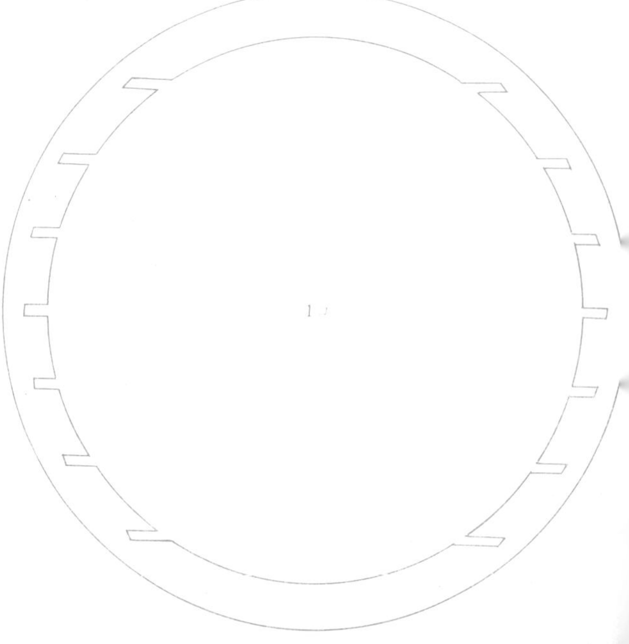
1コ